(be)known

Awaken Your Identity & Calling in Jesus

A 6-WEEK BIBLE STUDY

ALISSA CIRCLE
FOUNDER, BE TOGETHER CO.

Copyright © 2022 by Alissa Circle

ALL RIGHTS RESERVED

Published by Be Together Co.

Copyright and use of the curriculum template is retained by Brett Eastman.

Unless otherwise noted, all Scripture quotes are taken from Scripture taken from the New King James Version®. Copyright © 1982 by Thomas Nelson. Used by permission. All rights reserved.

Professional photography by Christina Wolfer at Christina Wolfer Photography.

 ISBN: 978-1-950007-73-8

Printed in the United States of America

contents

ENDORSEMENTS	4
INTRODUCTION	6
READER GUIDE	8

WEEK 1   12
The Invitation

WEEK 2   48
Identity

WEEK 3   88
Passion

WEEK 4   124
Uniquely Gifted

WEEK 5   162
Hope

WEEK 6   198
Sacred Love

APPENDICES

Name Chart	236	BeTogether Co.	244
Leader Guide	237	About the Author	248

endorsements

"Alissa Circle is a passionate and gifted teacher, writer and disciple maker. In her latest study she weaves personal testimony in with rich scripture in a way that sharpens and encourages. I've had the privilege of both sitting under her teaching and watching her serve in the most hidden places; she is a treasure and I know you'll be blessed by this study."

Beth Redman

"For the woman who has felt a loss of purpose and identity in Jesus, there is hope. Alissa delivers a beautiful message through scripture and insights that will draw you back to the feet of Jesus. This study will leave you with a renewed identity and deeper intimacy with Him."

Rebekah Lyons, *Bestselling Author, Rhythms of Renewal and You are Free*

"One of the greatest longings of every human heart is to be known. Alissa Circle beautifully curates and guides us on this most important journey to discover how each of us are seen, loved, and known by God. This six-week Bible Study will leave you encouraged and excited to spend more time in God's presence."

Tracy Wilde-Pace, *Speaker and Author of Finding the Lost Art of Empathy and Contentment: The Sacred Path to Loving the Life You Have*

"Alissa Circle is a dear friend of ours and is a woman with a contagious hunger for the Bible. The (Be) Known Bible Study will help women of all ages have a greater revelation of being fully known by God so that they can step into the deeper places of their walk with Him. You will finish this study with a tenacious faith and confidence in your God-given identity and purpose."

Mark & Rachelle Francey, *Lead Pastors, Oceans Church, Orange County, CA*

"As a pastor and women's ministry leader, I am always on the lookout for studies that are grounded in the Word, allow women to connect in a meaningful way and ultimately deepen their relationship with Jesus and Alissa's (Be) Known study does all this and more! This 6 week Bible study has everything you need to lead a group of women, from the study tool suggestions (I love some good pens) and the Worship playlist, to thought provoking group discussion points and homework that allows you to dig deeper on your own, (Be) Known will grow and stretch you as you become more intimate with our Savior in the process. Thank you Alissa for listening to the Holy Spirit and putting your study out in the world, I am excited to take the women of my church through this study in 2023."

Lisa Goins, *Author of Courageously Uncomfortable & Co-Lead Pastor of Faith Church, Tulsa, OK*

testimonials

"This Bible study has changed the trajectory of my confidence, my identity, my security and has given me a new passion, dreams and belief in myself that if Jesus is with me then I can conquer the giants and run after the dreams He has put in my heart. This study has changed my life, literally it has given me the confidence to do big, hard, scary things! Your obedience has brought me here!!! I am sooooo excited for the future and I haven't had that feeling in a long time!"

Chelsea Hoogenboom

"Alissa's Bible study brings a fresh wind to the heart. It reminds us that the journey is found in relationship not only with Jesus, but with those around us."

Robin Davis

"This Bible Study was like a breath of fresh air. It helped me discover different parts of God's character, led me to personal breakthroughs and self discoveries, and drew me into a beautiful community of women marked by vulnerability and depth... all prompted through delving into (Be) Known together. This is a study every woman would benefit from experiencing."

Jenn Tarbell

"Honestly, refreshing is the first word that comes to mind. It really gets you to dig deep and know God on a personal level. This is exactly what the world needs right now."

Molly Trotter

"God spoke so clearly to me through the (Be) Known study, revealing Himself in unexpected ways and calling attention to things He wanted to heal in me and dreams he wanted me to pursue with Him. Getting to journey through this study with other women provided a needed community of support and encouragement."

Erin Stone

"(Be) Known invites the reader to genuinely look and dive into the Father's perspective over their identity and heart. It allows time of reflection individually and with those who want to walk on this unique journey together."

Naomi Byrd

introduction

Dear Friend,

I am so thrilled that you decided to join me for the Be Known Bible Study. Writing this is the fulfillment of a calling and promise from God, and I can't wait for us to dive into His Word together. The Be Known study is born out of an understanding that God's greatest desire is for us to know Him and be known by Him.

It's no coincidence that when the Lord puts a message on your heart, it might encompass many stories, both personal and Biblical, but when you look back you can clearly see the overarching message. I wrote this Bible study out of obedience to my Heavenly Father. It began as a book until the Lord began to shape it into a Bible study. I love teaching. It's a passion of mine having been a lifelong learner. Studying the Bible and taking you all on a journey with me, at first, seemed like a big task. One I wasn't sure I had feet big enough to fill the shoes for. Isn't that the goodness of God that when He calls us to something, He gives us the tools we need to prepare for that calling. If we are obedient in the preparations, suddenly we begin to see Jesus move, like a swift wind that catches you off guard, but you lean into because it feels so good on your skin.

If I could take this whole Bible study and sum it up in one word; it would be ABIDE. To know who you are in Jesus, to have your identity be the foundation of who God says you are, you have to first understand the importance of sitting in His presence. Learning to hear His voice, coming into agreement with who He says you are. It's then that you can walk in your purpose or calling, using the gifts He's given you, in every season of your life. It's not only about abiding so that Jesus will accomplish all the goals you have for your life. You have to be willing to abide in all things, for all things and to all things.

Whether we are married, single, young kids, older kids, no kids, God has a purpose and plan for our lives. That is the overflow of what our lives can look like and how He can use us when we ABIDE in Him. The definition of Abide means "to remain." This word alone is written over 80 times in the Bible. If you've ever read the Bible start to finish, you will see 'remain' is written in the Bible even more times than the word Abide. Clearly God is saying to us, abide or remain in Me and what will I do? I will show you all the things you do not know (Jeremiah 33:3). I will give you the plans I have for, plans to prosper you (Jeremiah 29:11). I will give you an abundant life (John 10:10). When we abide in Him — we hear from Him, we know who Jesus is. We've created an intimate relationship with Him so that we can put our spiritual blinders on and focus on who He says we are, where he's taking us, what gifts He's going to use and how He's going to use them.

John 15:7 says, "if you remain in me and my Words remain in you, ask and you shall receive."1 Corinthians 13:13 says, "these three things remain, faith, hope and love, but the greatest of these is love." When we remain or abide in Jesus, our faith increases. It becomes abundant. And when our faith increases then we are able to live in this faith and in faith filled hope that what He has promised, He will bring to pass. We get to have the hope for the future He has for us and for the calling He has for our lives. Why? Because He loves us so much. That deep love for us is the reason He desires to be in relationship with us, so that we can go out and love others. To have greater kingdom impact and grow the kingdom of heaven.

This Be Known study is the first in a series of books and Bible studies designed around creating a community of women who can learn who they truly are in Christ and then turn to share the same message of truth and hope with others. Let's seek the Lord together, dream together, study His Word together, pray together, and then go together to expand the kingdom of God in our hurting world. It starts right here, right now in you and me, in our hearts. Let's go after Him. Let's dive in and Be Known!

Live Boldly in Him,

Alisa

Non-profit idea:
R.U.T.H. Ministries
*Reach Up To Heaven

using this workbook

Hello new friend, there are no words to express how excited I am that you've chosen to crack open the pages of this Bible study and dive into God's Word with me. This study is truly the result of devotion and obedience to the Holy Spirit. Every word on every page has been prayed over and my hope is that, as you read, the Lord meets you in a new and special way and you come away from these next six weeks transformed. Psalm 34:8 says, "Oh, taste and see that the Lord is good; Blessed is the man who trusts in Him!" In the next six weeks we're going to allow God to invite us into the secret place and remind us who He says we are, that we were each created on purpose for a purpose, with gifts already designed in the very fiber of our being, gifted to be used in every season. We're going to finish our time together sitting at the feet of Jesus at the cross, letting Him minister to us, pour out His love all over us so we can go out and confidently and boldly walk in the calling He has given each of us.

In this Bible study, we've included a section for taking notes on the video teaching and questions to guide your group time and response. While you do not need to watch the videos each week with your group, we do recommend it. They're such a beautiful extension to the study and homework each week. There are two tracks we recommend for you to follow: watch the video teaching and answer the questions for each week, or you can do the homework each week and walk your group through discussion of each day of homework, highlighting 2-3 thoughts from each day. We have included a leader guide in the appendix if your group decides to dive into the homework in your Bible study time each week. Our prayer is that your group will ~~chose~~ *choose* to go all in with Jesus over the next six weeks and watch the video teachings and complete the homework. We know life can get busy so please show up for Bible study even if you haven't completed the homework.

tools to help you have a great Bible study experience

1. Notice in the Table of Contents there are three sections: (1)Video Sessions; (2) Daily Homework; and (3) Appendix. Familiarize yourself with the Appendices. I've shared some great Bible Study tools, a leader guide and a worship playlist, filled with songs I've listened to over and over while writing this Bible study.

2. If you are facilitating/leading or co-leading a small group, the section Leader Guide, will be a helpful guide for your group if you decide to forego the videos and lead your group through discussion of the homework each week.

3. Use this workbook as a guide, not a straitjacket. If the group responds to the lesson in an unexpected but honest way, go with that. If you think of a better question than the next one in the lesson, ask it.

4. Pray before each session—for your group members, for your time together, and for wisdom and insights.

5. Read the outline for each session on the next pages so that you understand how the sessions will flow.

build your study tools bookshelf

Below are some recommended resources for our time studying together. You do not need all of these to complete the study, but I do highly recommend having a prayer journal on hand as you'll have prompts for journaling throughout the study. There's nothing more beautiful than coming before the Lord with your prayer requests and being able to go back and date the answered prayers in your journal. Some of the other tools I'm sharing with you include the various Bible translations I used when writing this study and other tools for leading your women's Bible study. To find all these tools, visit my website: **beknownbiblestudy.com/studytools**

outline of each week

if you use the video teachings

A typical group session for the (Be) Known study will include the following sections.

INTRODUCTION. Each lesson opens with a brief thought that will help you prepare for the session and get you thinking about the particular subject you will explore with your group. Make it a practice to read these before the session. You may want to have the group read them aloud.

COME TOGETHER. The foundation for spiritual growth is an intimate connection with God and His family. You build that connection by sharing your story with a few people who really know you and who earn your trust. This section includes some simple questions to get you talking—letting you share as much or as little of your story as you feel comfortable doing. Each session typically offers you two options.

You can get to know your whole group by using the icebreaker question(s), or you can check in with one or two group members for a deeper connection and encouragement in your spiritual journey.

GROW TOGETHER. In this section, you'll read the Bible and listen to teaching, in order to hear God's story—and begin to see how His story aligns with yours. When the study directs you, you will watch a short teaching segment. You'll then have an opportunity to read a passage of Scripture and discuss both the teaching and the text. You won't focus on accumulating information but on how you should live in light of the Word of God. We want to help you apply the insights from Scripture practically and creatively, from your heart as well as your head. At the end of the day, allowing the timeless truths from God's Word to transform our lives in Christ should be our greatest aim.

BE TOGETHER. God wants you to be a part of His Kingdom—to weave your story into His. That will mean change. It will require you to go His way rather than your own. This won't happen overnight, but it should happen steadily. By making small, simple choices, we can begin to change our direction. This is where the Bible's instructions to "be doers of the Word, not just hearers" (James 1:22) comes into play. Many people skip over this aspect of the Christian life because it's scary, relationally awkward, or simply too much work for their busy schedules. But Jesus wanted all of His disciples to know Him personally, carry out His commands, and help outsiders connect with Him. This doesn't necessarily mean preaching on street corners. It could mean welcoming newcomers, hosting a short-term group in your home, or walking through this study with a friend. In this study, you'll have an opportunity to go beyond Bible study to Biblical living. This section will also have a question or two that will challenge you to live out your faith by serving others, sharing your faith, and worshiping God.

overview of weekly homework

Remember, if you want to dive deep in God's Word you need to be willing to go all in. Sometimes that means a sacrifice of time as you let His words nourish you and bring about change. I promise you will never regret the time you spend in His presence.

Each day begins with a personal story. I cannot expect you to be vulnerable with each other through this study if I'm not always willing to share as well. My deepest desire is for you to feel as though we're sitting together in your living room, cup of coffee in hand, cozy blankets, studying God's Word together. We will then dive into the theme of each day together. This includes reading scripture, writing scripture and thoughtfully looking at how God wants to move in our lives each day. All five days end with two sections that will take you longer, but if you want to dive deeper with the Lord I encourage you to do them. Diving Deeper prompts are for you to sit with the Lord and look at areas of your life that He might be stretching you, pruning you, or challenging you to chase after Him in a new way. Then finally we end with a Posture of Prayer, with prayer journal prompts for the day. Prayer is the key to seeing shifts in your life, your business, your friendships and relationships. Revival in your life begins with prayer!

worship playlist

Worship music is like balm for the soul. I don't know if you feel the same, but the Lord speaks to me so often through worship songs. They've taken me through seasons of joy, sadness, the unknown, the desert and so many conversations with the Lord. Here is a playlist of songs that flowed on repeat as I wrote this Bible study and the book that will come alongside it.

- **Deep Dive -** SEU Worship
- **Who You Say I Am -** Hillsong Worship
- **O Come to the Altar -** Elevation Worship
- **Living Hope -** Phil Wickham
- **Holy Ground -** Passion
- **Closer -** Bethel Music
- **Real Thing -** Vertical Worship
- **I'm listening -** Chris McClarney
- **Way Maker -** Leland
- **Won't Look Back -** SEU Worship
- **My Hallelujah -** Bryan and Katie Torwalt
- **The Blessing -** Kari Jobe, Cody Carnes and Elevation Worship
- **Holy (Song of the Ages) -** The Belonging Co
- **Prophesy -** Influence Music
- **We Praise You -** Matt Redman
- **Rest on Us -** Upperroom
- **Make Room -** The Church will Sing, Elyssa Smith
- **Fall -** The Belonging Co
- **First Love -** Kari Jobe
- **Revival -** Jesus Culture & Chris McClarney
- **Lord Send Revival -** Hillsong Young & Free
- **House of Miracles -** Brandon Lake
- **Gold -** Jesus Culture
- **Breakthrough -** The Belonging Co
- **Fresh Wind -** Bethel Music & Brandon Lake
- **Promises -** Maverick City Music
- **Available -** Elevation Worship
- **Gratitude -** Brandon Lake
- **Jireh -** Elevation Worship & Maverick City Music
- **New Thing -** Hillsong Young & Free
- **Familiar Song -** SEU Worship & David Ryan Cook
- **Worthy of it All -** UPPERROOM

the invitation

WEEK ONE

Sweet Friends,

I can't believe we're beginning our first week diving into scripture together! Each day this week will have us confronting the truth about God, about ourselves, and about what He wants to do in our lives. Whether you have been following Jesus for a long time and have grown to a high level of maturity, you are a brand new Christian, or even someone who was once growing, but has lapsed in your walk with Him, this is going to be a powerful week. My prayer is that you will let God in and let Him have His way.

You're going to be reminded that God has already named you and He's inviting you into a deeper, more intimate relationship with Him. This week you're going to be encouraged to step out of where you are and move toward Jesus and His exciting purposes for your life. There might be moments where you begin to protest that your imperfections are too great, but take heart, Jesus' greatest desire wasn't to be in relationship with the perfect, but those who sought Him wholeheartedly. You're going to hear about the disciples, who were probably much more imperfect than you or I, and you'll confront both your doubts about your faith, and those areas where God is inviting you to trust in Him. Most importantly, you're going to walk away from this week with a stirring for a deeper relationship with your Heavenly Father - because He sees you and He wants you to be known by Him.

I'm confident that this week will kick us off powerfully and put us in a great position to BE KNOWN!

LIVE BOLDLY IN HIM,

Alisia

group discussion

Open with a time of worship together. There's a worship playlist in the appendix if you need some help picking out a song.

introduction

How do you feel about receiving invitations? Do you well up with excitement? Do you experience a sudden sense of dread? I guess it really depends on who is inviting you and what you're being invited to. God is inviting you to abide in Him. It's a call to Be, not just a call to Do. How does that make you feel?

come together

Each of us has a story. The events of our life—good, bad, wonderful or challenging— have shaped who we are. God knows your story, and He intends to redeem it—to use every struggle and every joy to ultimately bring you to Himself. When we share our stories with others, we give them the opportunity to see God at work.

When we share our stories, we also realize we are not alone—that we have common experiences and thoughts, and that others can understand what we are going through. Your story can encourage someone else, and telling it can lead to a path of freedom for you and for those you share it with.

Open your group with prayer.

If your group is new, welcome newcomers. Introduce everyone—you may even want to have name tags for your first meeting.

ice breaker questions

We recommend picking one. It can be one of ours, or one of your own. Have each woman in the group take a moment to answer.

- Think about an invitation you were really excited to receive. Why were you excited about it?
- On a scale from 1 to 10 with self-care being 1 and busyness being 10, where would you place yourself?

WEEK 1 | THE INVITATION

watch video session 1

beknownbiblestudy.com/videos

group discussion

grow together

Read John 15:7

"If you abide in me, and my words abide in you, you will ask what you desire and it shall be done for you."

- What do you find comforting about the idea of abiding?
- What do you find challenging about the idea of abiding?

Have someone Read Matthew 14:22-23

- If you were on that boat with the disciples, how would you have felt about the storm and seeing Jesus walking on the water?
- Would you have jumped out of the boat to walk on water like Peter? Why or why not?

be together

God wants you to be part of His kingdom—to weave your story into His. That will mean change—to go His way rather than your own. This won't happen overnight, but it should happen steadily. By starting with small, simple choices, we begin to change our direction. The Holy Spirit helps us along the way—giving us gifts to serve the body, offering us insights into scripture, and challenging us to love not only those around us but those far from God.

In this section, talk about how you will apply the wisdom you've learned from the teaching and Bible study. Then think about practical steps you can take in the coming week to live out what you've learned.

- Describe a time in your life where you took a huge leap of faith.
- What is God calling you to that just seems impossible right now?
- When you think of your relationship with God, what's keeping you in the boat spiritually?

Ask, "How can we pray for you this week?" Invite everyone to share, but don't force the issue. Be sure to write prayer requests in your prayer journal. Don't have one. You can grab one of mine from the Bible Study Bookshelf located in the appendix. Be sure to encourage the women to dive into the homework each week. It's an important part of our Spiritual growth.

Close your meeting with prayer.

WEEK 1

daily study

DAY ONE

In my teen years I had always disliked my name. No one else shared it. I could never find it spelled correctly on souvenirs, and people never said it correctly. Inevitably someone would always pronounce it al-eee-sa or ali-cia. At one point, I wanted to change my name to Elizabeth because it seemed so much more sophisticated, with so many potential nicknames, and less likelihood of mispronunciation. I remember my parents sharing with me at one point that they had originally picked out the name Mara for me. Which, by the way, means bitter. I somehow managed to avoid this name, but still found myself bitter about the name they had chosen in its place. For so many years I never felt it suited me. I couldn't see the purpose behind my name. God had named me Alissa with an "i", not a "y" so I would know I was created wholly and uniquely. One day in the future He would use me to speak His truth. It would take years for me to embrace my name, but now I cherish its uniqueness

Have you ever looked up the meaning of your name online? I remember the first time I opened a book of names in a bookstore to scan the pages for my name. Don't laugh. This was before the glorious days of Google. Anyone else remember those days? As my finger traced down the names under 'A,' I reached my own. The word "truthful" stared back at me from the page. As an adult I began

WEEK 1 | THE INVITATION

searching for the meaning of my name once again. There sitting in front of me, brightly shining on the screen in a way I couldn't miss was, "Alissa means truthful and noble." Noble! Friends, I tried to change my name in middle school to make it sound more noble, yet God had given me that name already. My favorite part? In Hebrew, my name is translated to "Joy." I wish I could describe the feelings the Lord brought to the surface. So much was redeemed for me in that moment.

HE PICKED YOUR NAME

my name is... **Amina Ruth**

which means... **honest, faithful friend**

Take a moment to look up your name online.

What does your name mean?
Amina → origin is Arabic and means trustworthy, loyal or faithful. Ruth → in Hebrew, means friend. Root word is re'ut.

For some, your name might have a Biblical meaning.

What is yours?
Amina was the name of the prophet Muhammad. Ruth is the 8th book of the Bible (OT) & one of only two books named for 9.

What is significant about your name to you?
My father named me Amina because he was Muslim. My mother named me Ruth (middle name) after herself and my great aunt.

What are some initial thoughts and feelings that come up for you when you read the meaning of your name?
Amina is cultural + ethnic. I haven't always embraced it. I feel like people can make assumptions about me based on my name alone. I've also not embraced Ruth until I became familiar with the Biblical story.

What are some names you've given yourself or others have given you? For me, some of these names are synonymous with insecurities I have carried.

No matter whether you like or resonate with the meaning of your name, it's important for you to know God knew you before you were born and before you were named. There was no doubt in His mind as He formed you so intricately in your mother's womb, who you would be. He whispered your name, laying claim to you before you were even a thought in your parents' mind. There's something so profound in knowing that we were created with such purpose and precision. There wasn't a detail He didn't consider-- no base He didn't cover. Jesus did this so we would know without a second thought we are His. You may associate your name with hardship or pain, but God wants to heal you and help you to fully embrace who you are and how He created you. Friend, Jesus wants you to know that every time Jesus calls your name, He's speaking over you with His love.

Looking back at the story of creation we see God's intention and detail. Each day He created and at the end of that day, He called it good. The word good is used for the first time in Genesis 1:4. The Hebrew word means to be pleasing, joyful, and favorable. In Genesis chapter one, at the end of each day, we see God call what He has created good, this includes the creation of man and woman. Every detail of creation knows its name because it knows its creator. Just like each day as God finished creating and called it good and pleasing, this includes you, sister. Come join me in Genesis and let's look at the intentionality of our Heavenly Father is together.

Genesis 1:3-10 (NKJV)

"Then God said, "Let there be _____"; and there was _____. And God saw that the light was good; and He separated light from the darkness. God called the light _____, and the darkness He called _____. And there was evening, and there was morning - the first day. Then God said, "Let there be a _____ between the waters to separate water from water. So God made the _____ and separated the water under the vault from water above it and it was so. God called the vault _____. And there was evening, and there was morning - the second day. And God said, "Let the water under the sky be gathered to one place, and let dry ground appear." And it was so. God called the dry ground _____, and the gathered waters he called _____. And God saw that it was good."

WEEK 1 | THE INVITATION

Every part of creation was called by name, and they knew they were His. Just as Jesus calls you, friend, by name because you are His. His precious daughter, who He loves and cherishes beyond what you could ever imagine. God creating, naming, and calling us to be in relationship with Him is nothing new. It existed all the way back to creation.

What does "being known" mean to you? *Having someone being familiar with the good and bad of a person, with the intimate details, "secrets," insecurities etc. It's about being seen and being given the space to be your authentic self.*

Is it difficult for you to believe that you were created on purpose for a purpose? Why or why not? *It is not difficult for me to believe. I feel in my soul + spirit that God created me for "more." I believe that I've been destined for greatness, although I don't necessarily know the specific intent or purpose - or how to execute it.*

Over the course of the next six weeks, we're going to dive into the deep with Jesus. To accept His invitation to fully embrace who He is and allow him to speak into us and over us who we are and how intricately we've been created. To be KNOWN by Him so we can fully lean into His calling on our lives, using the gifts He's given us in every season of our lives. Thank you, Jesus, we serve a God who wants to know us, use us, and send us out to multiply His kingdom. My prayer is that in our time together we can allow the Lord to heal us, refine us and restore us so we can testify to His goodness! Amen?!

The call to come and experience the fullness of what a life walking with Jesus looks like goes back to when God created Adam and Eve.

Read Genesis 1:26-31; 2:18-24

God creates the heavens and the earth, separates darkness from light, creates land and sea, birds of the air, fish of the sea, animals of the land. He gives them all freedom to enjoy the fruit of His creation, but He doesn't stop there. God values relationships and the overflow of that desire is He creates man and woman.

> Then God said, "Let us make mankind in our image, in our likeness, so that they may rule over the fish in the sea and the birds in the sky, over the livestock and all the wild animals, and over all the creatures that move along the ground."
>
> *Genesis 1:26*

What is the meaning of Adam's name? (Hint: Gen. 2:20) _____

What is the meaning of Eve's name? (Hint: Gen 3:20) _____

We are invited into the story of God's creation. Why? Because He wants us to know that it didn't begin and end with Adam and Eve. Despite the fall in the garden as a result of Adam and Eve's sin, God did not give up humanity He didn't, in that moment, decide that He no longer wanted to create new life. In fact, we see the opposite throughout the word of God. The invitation to come and sit in His presence to allow Him to pour His love into you and over you has not changed. Throughout the Old Testament we see Him call people to turn away from their old ways repeatedly and let Him rename them.

That's the first real invitation. Friend, He has called you by name, He desires to be in a relationship with you. Are you willing to see yourself as God sees you?

Diving Deeper

Did looking at your name, names you've given yourself and others have given you bring up anything unexpected for you? What areas are you still struggling to see God's hand in your life? What do you need to let go of today and allow Him to transform so you can open your heart to all that He has for you?

_____
_____
_____
_____
_____
_____
_____
_____
_____

WEEK 1 | THE INVITATION

When we approach the throne with a heart shift, casting off the names the world has given us and clothing ourselves in who God says we are, we can fully experience the newness that God wants to do in our lives. Tomorrow, we're going to dive right in, headfirst into the invitation Jesus offers to "Come," as we look at the story in Matthew 14 of Peter walking on water. It is one of my favorite stories in the New Testament, and though it's one we've all heard before, I'm believing God is going to breathe new meaning into it for you. We must first understand and recognize the truth that we were created by a loving God, who desires to have an intimate relationship with us. Are you ready to Be Known?

Posture of Prayer

Take a few moments to journal and thank Jesus for so intricately creating you and naming you. Share any insecurities you've held onto and let them go. Allow Him to prepare your heart as you journal and pray to be seen and known by Him. The last few years the Lord has been healing me of insecurities I've held onto for so long -- Unworthiness, timidity, ill-equipped. All names I've spoken over myself or allowed others to speak over me. My prayer is that as you journal and pray, our Heavenly Father will begin to break the ones you've been carrying off of you.

(BE)KNOWN

DAY TWO

I accepted Jesus when I was three years old. My mom was baking chocolate chip cookies in the kitchen of our home in Kaneohe, HI. The sweet smell permeated our home. With the sound of the mixer whirling, I came to her boldly and told her I needed Jesus in my life. I dropped to my knees at the edge of the kitchen and asked Jesus to come into my heart and be my forever friend. God was already talking to me, even from a young age. I would grow up to rededicate my life to Jesus as a teenager, but for so many years I was a lukewarm believer. Of course, if you were to point that out to me, I would adamantly deny it, declaring that I go to church, participate in Bible study, and send my kids to a Christian school. I was content with going through the motions, fitting the Holy Spirit into pockets of my day, but not fully inviting Him into all of it. I had a successful career, CEO of my own multi-million dollar business, but in the back of my mind I felt that God would never use me to multiply His kingdom. I became content to just work hard to earn money to give to others so they could do it on my behalf.

WEEK 1 | THE INVITATION

Oh, the lies we let the enemy speak in our ear. First, that our home or our marketplace can't be our ministry. Second, that you're only truly discipling when you're speaking to hundreds of thousands of people night after night about Jesus, leading a church or Bible study, or running a nonprofit in a third world country. Here's the truth friend, your ministry and your platform are right where you're sitting right now. It's smack in the middle of your workplace, your home, your marriage, your parenting, your leadership, your writing, and your sermon preparation.. When the pandemic hit, I found myself floundering and so I went to the one place I knew I'd find my footing, --the feet of Jesus. I began reading His word, worshiping, journaling my prayers, and inviting the Holy Spirit in every part of my life. I sat at Jesus' feet and let Him rename me: Alissa, noble daughter of the most high king, created and anointed by God to serve and multiply His kingdom, through speaking truth in love.

PROMPTING LEADS TO PREPERATION

Before we go any further today, it's important that we take captive any thoughts that hold us back from knowing and believing we're called to be used by God. When you think of names you've given yourself or allowed others to give you, which ones are still stuck with you today? (inadequate, failure, shy, not good at…) You can list them in the margin.

names I have given myself

What holds you back from believing God has a calling on your life?

What would it look like to be so intentional about our relationship with Jesus, that when He calls us into something, we don't first look outward, but we look upward and begin asking Him for the strength to be obedient? This means taking the time to learn how to hear His voice, lean into what He's saying, and then take steps that move you into a space of, "God, I trust you more, and therefore, help me to walk in this calling."

> I will give you every place where you set your foot, as I promised Moses.
>
> *Joshua 1:3*

Let's read Joshua 1:1-18 together.

Take a minute to look up Joshua's name, what does it mean? _____
(Let's add it to our chart on page 236.)

It's no coincidence that God chose to use a man named Joshua, who was trained up under Moses, to deliver His people into the land He promised them. We read about many promises God made, but He didn't always just snap His fingers and make it all happen quick and easy, although I'm sure the grumbling Israelites would've liked that. Somedays I would really like it that way, can I get an amen?! As we begin the book of Joshua, the Israelites learn that Moses has died and God is calling Joshua up to the front lines. He will bring the Israelites from wandering in the wilderness to the promise land.

In Joshua 1: 3-5, God makes multiple promises, what are they?

1. _____
2. _____
3. _____
4. _____
5. _____

This isn't the first time the Israelites have faced a body of water blocking them from their deliverance. While none of them experienced crossing the Red Sea because of the disobedience of the generation before them (Numbers 14:29-22, they would've heard stories passed down from their parents about God using Moses to part the waters so they could escape captivity in Egypt. I wonder if it's the reminder of God's faithfulness back in Egypt that elevates their faith in that moment to follow the leadership of Joshua. The priests gather the ark of the covenant, put their feet into the water, which parted, making a pathway of dry land for the Israelites to cross.

What do you think was going through their minds when Joshua told them that the promise was just on the other side of the Jordan, and they only need to cross it to take hold of it?

WEEK 1 | THE INVITATION

God told Joshua He would deliver on the promise He made Moses. He would bring that promise to pass everywhere they set foot. God had used the years Joshua had served under Moses' leadership to prepare him for this moment. Oftentimes, when we feel the Lord's prompting there is a preparation, perhaps even a wandering in the desert that needs to happen first. If you can lean on God when it feels like nothing is happening and still stand on the promise, then you will lean on God when door after door is flinging wide open in front of you.

Joshua chapter one isn't the first time God asks His people to look to Him, place their trust solely in Him, and step into the promise He has for them. Let's look at a few other examples together. The first one is filled out for you.

READ	WHO	ACTION	PROMISE
Joshua 4	Joshua	Step into the Jordan and God would part the waters	Enter the promised land
Genesis 6:9-22			
Exodus 14:21-22			
Joshua 2:2; 6-13			
Joshua 6:15-20			

Which passage elevated your level of faith today to step into a promise God has spoken over you? _____

Diving Deeper

What promises has the Lord been whispering in your ear? Have you felt as though you've been walking in the wilderness rather than walking in your calling? In what ways do you think the Lord is using this season as a season of preparation?

_____

_____

_____

_____

_____

_____

_____

_____

There are miracles in the movement, friends! I don't know about you, but this feels both exciting and terrifying to me. What if I make the wrong moves? I know that our Heavenly Father designed us on purpose and for a purpose. We were created to stand up, step out, and live a life with Him. He has so many promises in store for us. In our lifetime we will probably never know the magnitude of all that He has planned for our lives. Often when we read the Bible, we believe the lies that signs, wonders, and miracles were for then. The powerful moves of God were reserved for men like Joshua, Noah, Moses, David, Esther, Deborah, Peter, Paul, and others back then, but my friend, that is simply not true. God is still in the midst of the miraculous today. It's up to us to decide if we want to live in the miraculous with Him.

Posture of Prayer

Take some time today to journal and let go of areas of your life that you've held back from being fully used by Him. Ask Him to begin to show you ways He wants to use you, right where you are, where you've allowed your circumstances to let you believe you can't be used by God in this season. Spend some time thanking Him for His goodness and holding tight to His promises for your life.

DAY THREE

I love going to the gym. It wasn't always like that. I used to loathe any kind of workout setting. When I walked in all I could see was what I wasn't. I wasn't the one in a cute, matching workout outfit. I wasn't the one who could work out and look like they glistened. I certainly wasn't the one who made it through at a level 10 for the whole 45 minutes. Halfway through the workout the voice in my head was louder than the trainer. My whole body was the color of a bright tomato waiting to be plucked. I was puffing so loudly I was disturbing my neighbors. More than once, I thought why am I paying for this? I'm paying to be tortured and made to feel inadequate. Every time someone would smile at me during the workout, I felt their pity. It was like I could feel the weight of their judgment slithering down me like a snake through the grass.

Then, as time passed, I found myself not being as winded. I started hearing the voice of the trainer over my own. I looked forward to going because I liked how I felt afterwards. I was seeing the results of my hard work. I began learning people's names. When they smiled at me, I smiled back. I was the one making myself feel inadequate by telling myself lies before someone else had the chance to point their judgment at me. You can't tell me something I've already told myself. I placed labels on myself to use as a shield when I should've seen my fitness journey as just that -- my own. It wasn't a journey of comparison. It wasn't about how I looked next to others who have been working out longer to determine how well my workout would go. A lost sense of identity can happen anywhere, anytime, and about anything. It creeps up on you from behind, crawls up your back, and slithers into your ear.

HIS INVITATION IS INTENTIONAL

In the last couple days, we visited the very beginning of creation to help us stand firm in the knowledge that God created us all with purpose. It's important to know that creation didn't just spontaneously happen. The same creator (God) who created the heavens and the earth (Genesis 1) and all that lives and roams in it, who, with intention, named them all, is the same creator who loves you, named you, and knows you. His greatest desire is for you to know who you are in Him. Today we're diving into the New Testament and looking at what the call to come dive headfirst into God's presence with a deep desire to be known and used by Him means.

Let's read Luke 5:1-10.

Jesus was intentional in choosing his disciples. He wasn't looking for people of wealth or nobility, perfection or well-connected in society. He chose ordinary people, just like you and me. If God thought the coming of Jesus would've had a greater impact if He had been born a king or ruler, He had all authority to make that happen. Yet, God, in His goodness, knew that Jesus' impact would be greater if His life mirrored ours. He was born to young parents, raised with brothers and sisters, had chores and responsibilities, and had a job (He was a carpenter). His formal ministry didn't begin until he was 30 years old (John 2).

How does knowing that Jesus grew up with so many of the same experiences and expectations we did help you to relate to Him better? What thoughts or feelings keep you from thinking Jesus knows you and understands what you're going through?

Jesus chose us in spite of our imperfections and even our lack of faith.

As Jesus came to the edge of the Lake of Gennesaret, surrounded by crowds of people listening to the word of God, He saw Simon, James, and John washing their nets on the shore. It was important to wash out the nets with fresh water, tie off any tears, and stretch the nets. Otherwise, the water and dredge over time would harden the nets, so they would not stay loose to hold the fish.

What time of day was it? _____

The Lake of Gennesaret is an ancient reference Luke uses here to talk about the Sea of Galilee. It's a freshwater lake in Israel that is 13 miles long and seven miles wide. It's not a large lake, but it was a huge food source for people in that area. It is believed that in Jesus' time there were hundreds of men who owned fishing boats and actively caught fish for a living. Simon Peter and Andrew, along with James and John are fishermen. They had just finished an entire night of fishing and had caught nothing. We find them on the shore cleaning and stretching their nets to prepare them to hang to dry and be ready for the next night of fishing.

WEEK 1 | THE INVITATION

Jesus came on the scene with a crowd following close behind Him. He climbed into their boat and began preaching. He used this moment to demonstrate to the people metaphorically what it means to be "fishers of men."

Re-read Luke 5:4

What does Jesus ask Simon Peter to do? _____

What feelings or emotions might've been going through the minds of Simon. James and John when Jesus says this?

What I love so much about this passage is not what Jesus asks Peter to do, or even how he must've been feeling when Jesus asked him to take his boat and his nets back into the water and cast them, it's his response. Yes, he begins by saying they fished all night and caught nothing, but then he says…

Luke 5:4b (NIV)

"But because _____ say so, I will _____ _____ the nets."

Simon chooses a posture of obedience to what Jesus is asking. This wasn't the first time Simon Peter stepped out in obedience. This moment is significant because the fishermen would fish on the Sea of Galilee at night when the temperature was cooler, making the fish more likely to come closer to the surface to feed and swim. When Jesus told Simon Peter to cast his nets in the water again, it's daytime. The sun had warmed the water's surface. Simon Peter knew the fish would've moved to deeper, cooler waters.

The men cast their nets into the deeper water and suddenly fish were jumping left and right into their nets. They caught so many fish (using the same nets that had been washed, cleaned, and stretched) that those same nets began to tear under the weight of the fish. The men in the boat called for the help of other fishing boats nearby to help bear the weight and reel in the nets. The fish kept swimming into the nets until it seemed as though the boats would sink from the weight of the fish.

If you were part of the crowd that had been following Jesus, what would be going through your mind watching this all unfold?

Jesus knew he was going to call those men that day to come and follow him, so He provided over and above their needs. Why? So, they would know that by following Him, all they would ever need would be provided and taken care of. Peter, James, and John were equally amazed and afraid of Jesus, having just experienced such a profound miracle. Not a fear that Jesus had come to do harm, but an awe and reverence. Who is this man? Is He the Messiah they had heard about all our lives?

Jesus said to them, "Don't be afraid, from now on you will catch men." (vs. 11) They received an invitation to come and follow Jesus, simultaneously eliminating any question in their mind if they would be taken care of should they leave it all behind and go.

How has Jesus provided for your needs?

This is one of many defining moments that makes Jesus' changing of Simon's name so significant. Simon is a Greek name meaning, "he has heard." Later he is referred to as Simon Peter and then most commonly, as Peter, after he became one of Jesus' disciples. Peter according to Matthew 16:18 means, "rock" Here we see a literal renaming of Simon to Peter, but God doesn't always physically rename us. In the same way Jesus gives Simon a new name, He does that for each of you as well. It may not be outward, but He does give you a new name when you choose to follow Him above all else. He calls you His.

WEEK 1 | THE INVITATION

There will be times Jesus wants to clean us and stretch us like the disciples would their fishing nets. Other times, Jesus simply asks us to come, launch into the deep, and do something unexpected like when He asked the disciples to cast their nets after a night of fishing with no catch. It's an open invitation to watch what God can do.

Diving Deeper

What are areas of your life that you need Jesus to come in and clean out? Why have you been unwilling to let it go, maybe for fear of letting go, surrendering the control of what you've been holding on to? Where is Jesus wanting to stretch you and prepare you for launch?

_____
_____
_____
_____
_____
_____
_____

There are always going to be moments where we feel like the Lord is washing us down. Maybe some days, it feels more like a dousing. Or maybe He's stretching you, plucking out the seaweed. It can feel laborious, or even frustrating, but know that Jesus' love for you is so vast that anytime He's working on you it's because He's calling you higher, into something greater than where you're standing right now. He needs you to be ready. Be willing to do the work, so He can clear spaces where He wants to fill.

Posture of Prayer

Take a few minutes in your journal to talk to Jesus about those areas you need to give over control and allow Him to come in and clean and stretch you. Let Him know you are ready to be fully used by Him, for whatever He has planned for your life. Tell Him how grateful you are that He has called you and has a plan for your life.

(BE)KNOWN

DAY FOUR

It had been almost a year since I had started writing my book, (Be) Known, in obedience to a dream and a calling I felt the Lord so strongly give me in 2019, both in my time with Him and through the exhortations of others. Yet here I was, feeling stuck. Unseen. Unknown. Again. The words were coming, achingly slow. One morning, I heard the Lord say, "Why are you still holding onto what you think I'm not doing, and not looking at all I've already begun to do? Do you not see it? I have brought you into a new thing (Isaiah 43:19), why are you choosing to look to your left and to your right? Stand strong in the new identity I've given you. In your obedience to me, I will continue to open doors for you to walk on the water." This was such a pivotal moment for me. When we learn to incline our ears to Jesus' thoughts about us and His plans for our lives, we don't get caught up in trivial thing, We keep our focus on Him.

When your identity is centered in what Jesus says about you, then you will have those moments with Him often. I remember finding my way over and over to a passage

WEEK 1 | THE INVITATION

in Matthew 14, only it felt as though the words were taking on new form, lifting off the page, being highlighted in a new way. As I read, I saw myself in Matthew, but I knew God was nudging me to boldly step out like Peter. I'm positive you know what story I'm talking about. So much was holding me back from embracing all that Jesus had for me. I still felt I was unworthy to receive it. I still felt like I wasn't the right person for the job. That thought broke me. How much time had I let drift by believing that dreams were meant for dreaming, but never doing? How often had I questioned God's plan for my life to the point that my doubts became a roadblock?

COME AND EXPERIENCE

What doubts in your life have become a roadblock for you?

Read Matthew 14:22-33

The disciples had just watched Jesus perform a miracle-- feeding over 15,000 people (including men, women, and children) from five loaves and two fish. Just imagine what it must've been like to be there that day. To bear witness to that many people traveling from all over the country to hear Jesus speak and receive an unexpected miracle. I wonder how many miracles the crowd saw that day? How many healings? Deliverances?

Jesus did what He often did after a day of teaching and performing miracles, He retreated to pray. This time He made the disciples get in the boat and go on ahead without Him. The word "make," in this passage is a strong word, meaning "to compel." Some translations use the word "directed" (Amplified Bible) or "constrained" (KJV) to point out Jesus' instance that the disciples get in the boat and go. There was an urgency in Jesus' voice to remove the disciples from the crowd.

> *"Lord, if it's you," Peter replied, tell me to come to you on the water."*
> *"Come," he said.*
>
> *Matthew 14:28*

Read John 6:14-16

Why was Jesus making the disciples get in the boat and keep going?

Go back and review Matthew 14:22-34, then read Mark 6:45-52, John 6:16-21

List out some similarities between these 3 accounts of Jesus walking on the water.

What is the biggest difference?

The storm kept blowing into the very early morning. Each account says it was the fourth watch, which is somewhere between 3-6 a.m., the disciples were 3-4 miles offshore. They had been battling a storm.

With the winds and storm brewing around them, all at once there was a new commotion in the boat. Someone called out in confusion that they saw a ghost walking on the water.

Jesus called out to them, "Do not be afraid, take courage. I am here!"

Peter's voice is then heard calling out to Jesus. "Lord, if it's really you, tell me to come to you, walking on the water."

"Come." Jesus replied.

One word, but even I realize just how much meaning is packed into that one word. This one word invitation holds such magnitude. It seems like a simple request, but in reality, it's packed with unknowns and self-doubts.

When Jesus called out to the disciples in the boat, we don't hear Him say, "Peter, come." He responded simply with one word, "Come." A beautiful,

WEEK 1 | THE INVITATION

open invitation to everyone who believed what He had for them was far better, far greater than what was in the boat.

- More freedom... (2 Corinthians 3:17)
- More purpose... (Ephesians 2:10)
- More abundance ... (John 10:10)

Matthew's account of the disciples getting caught in the storm is my favorite of all the gospel accounts. Here we get the full details of what happened on the boat early that morning. Each time I read this story I picture Peter and Matthew at the bow of the boat, engaging with Jesus as the rest of the disciples in the back of the boat. This very same story is mentioned in the book of Luke and John, but neither one mentions the interaction between Peter and Jesus that led to Peter stepping out on the water. The experience must've impacted Matthew more than we give credit for because it's the only gospel that talks about Jesus inviting them to come out on the water.

What do you think is going through Matthew's mind? If you were him, standing there with Peter, what would you be saying to Peter?

Take a moment and look up the meaning of Matthew's name: _____
(add to our chart on page 236)

I try to imagine myself on the boat that day. No land in sight, middle of the night, tired, wet, and battling the wind and waves of a storm, and in the distance, a man comes in the midst of the storm and He's walking on the water. It's no wonder their first inclination is that they must be seeing a ghost. After all, who can walk on water, much less with waves crashing around you? Jesus knew that His disciples would be weary in the storm and wondering why Jesus had left them and so He went to them. He could have calmed the storm from the shore. He could've appeared on the boat, or even come alongside them in another boat, but He chose to demonstrate His power and authority by walking out on the water to meet His disciples. We see this beautiful interaction between Him and Peter.

In this moment Jesus reminds them of who He is... the great I AM.

- He speaks a promise (v. 27)
- Offers an invitation (v. 29)
- Invites them to participate in a miracle (v. 29)

Jesus tells them not to fear. "Do not fear" is written in the Bible 365 times! God never intended for us to walk this life on earth alone. He speaks this promise over and over so we can be reminded that He is I AM, with all authority, dominion, and power, which He left with us when He rose to Heaven after His death. I love how He declares who He is, tells them not to be afraid, and beautifully invites them into a deeper relationship with Him.

Come

Trust me. Do not be afraid. Step out into the deep. I've got you. Have courage. We're going to do this together. Yes, the storm might feel like it's raging, some days it might seem like it's more than you can handle, but fear not. Keep your eyes on me. Your maker. Creator of the heavens and earth. Commander over this ocean and the storms in your life. I will make a way.

His invitation was for all the disciples in the boat. Yes, we see Jesus responding to Peter, but if He had truly meant the invitation to be for one, He would've said, "Peter, come." Yet He responds with one word. The conversation must've impacted Matthew so profoundly that He shared it in his writing to remind us not to miss the invitation to participate in all that Jesus has for us. It's so much more than we could ever imagine or plan for ourselves.

I wonder sometimes if Matthew felt He missed out on the opportunity that day to step into the deep with Jesus, but we're going to dive into that more tomorrow.

WEEK 1 | THE INVITATION

Diving Deeper

What fears have been holding you back from truly stepping in the deep with Jesus? Have you felt like you missed an opportunity and there won't be another one? Or it's too late to step out onto the water? Do you need to see a transformation or a miracle in your life today?

_____
_____
_____
_____
_____
_____
_____
_____
_____
_____

God has something so special for you. It's not a coincidence that you picked up this Bible study. He's ready to help you take that next step to cast off what's holding you back, and instead of leaning out of the boat to watch someone else step out, it's going to be you. In Jesus name, my prayer is that you will feel a new washing of His presence and begin to answer that stirring in your heart to serve God right where he's planted you. Even in the unexpected places, in your home, in your family, in your friendships, and in your job.

Posture of Prayer

Take a few minutes and ask the Lord to show you areas of your life where you need to let go of fear. Acknowledge ways that He has been "I AM" in your life and your rock in the storm. Sit with Him and just empty your mind of everything but Jesus, and then listen for His voice. What is He telling you? What miracles do you need to see happen in your life? Declare His victory over all of them.

DAY FIVE

I grew up in a Christian home. Both of my parents were believers and for many of those years, their faith, and their relationship with Jesus, was, by default, mine as well. I might have accepted Jesus when I was three but understanding how to own my faith came much later for me. Growing up I had many holy encounters with God, but I never saw myself being used by Him. I always shied away from sharing my faith with others. My friends knew I went to church and loved Jesus, many of them attended youth group at my house, but I didn't go out of my way to talk about my love for Jesus with people around me. I was content to let others do the "work" of the kingdom. I was happy to fade into the background and claim a relationship with Jesus, while being unworried about bearing any fruit from it. Truth be told, I felt so lost in my teenage years. I looked for my identity in boys and relationships. I invited boys to church and youth group so I could show off my relationship with Jesus because I always felt more justified in going out with them if they were going to church with me. Finally, I realized the relationships still left me feeling empty, and then we would part ways, only to have many of them not return to church.

WEEK 1 | THE INVITATION

For many years I carried the guilt of how many of those young men I dated might never meet Jesus or could've met Jesus so much sooner, had I not selfishly interfered. Yet, we serve a God who redeems us and all that we perceive as lost. His compassion and mercy meet us where we are. Jesus wipes the slate clean and, never remembers past sins. We begin anew. Some days I still find it so overwhelming that the Lord chooses even those who found themselves lost at some point to multiply His kingdom. There is no such thing as a perfect disciple, but there is one with a willing heart. My friend, I'm here to tell you there is a difference!

GOD'S DREAMS FOR US ARE BIGGER

Read Isaiah 43:18-19

Write the passage below.

Jesus is the WAY, the TRUTH, and the LIFE (John 14:6). When He says He will make a way, He means, with Him all things are possible (Matthew 19:26). Isaiah 43 reminds us that just as God doesn't look back, He doesn't desire for us to dwell in our past either. It doesn't matter what you let control your life yesterday, He only cares about how you're choosing to follow Him today!

Read Jeremiah 33:3

In the margin, re-write it in your own words. When was the last time you took some time and asked the Lord to speak words of affirmation over you?

Jeremiah 33:3

Look back at Matthew 14:22-32.

At this point in Jesus' ministry, He had called all 12 disciples. When Jesus made the disciples get into the boat and go ahead of him, we know they're all together. Despite being in a boat together having just witnessed an incredible miracle, one that directly confirmed God's provision, we need to remember that they're all young boys. Late teens and early 20's. They were physically young, but they were also young in their faith.

Where are you in your faith journey?

|—————————————————————————————|

STILL SEEKING   MATURE

We can proclaim that our relationship with Jesus goes through ebbs and flows, but the truth is, the more time we spend seeking Him and spending time in His word, we mature in our faith. There are over 7,000 promises in the Word of God. The more we read them, the more we can stand on them during seasons of our life we need them the most. Maybe, you're reading this Bible study and you're desperate to see God move in your life. You're where Peter was as he stood on the edge of the boat that morning.

Matthew 14:28

"Lord, _____ you, _____ me to come to you on the water." - Matthew 14:28

This is a word for somebody today, amen! As you're reading this, how are you identifying with Matthew in those moments before Peter stepped out of the boat? You can feel that same tension. Jesus, in this moment, is challenging their entire belief system. Yes, they had seen Jesus perform miracles, but could they also have the power and authority to experience it for themselves. Peter might've been the one to say the words aloud, "Lord, if it really is you, call me...," but I can't help but wonder if Matthew was thinking them. Do you think so too? You're in the right company.

Do you need a moment like this with Jesus?

WEEK 1 | THE INVITATION

Where do you need to see Jesus in your life today? What new thing do you feel Him stirring in your heart, yet you're unable to take the step out on the water?

Friend, can I just tell you, Jesus wants us all to be like Peter. He's calling all of us to a unique calling in alignment with His purpose for our lives. When we establish our identity in Him, we will not only hear when He calls but we will step out of the boat. Some of you are stuck in a belief system that God uses others, but He can't, won't, or would never use you. There is nothing further from the truth.

In what ways have you identified with Matthew in your life?

What do you think is the biggest difference between Matthew and Peter in this moment?

> When we establish our identity in Him, we will not only hear when He calls but we will step out on the boat.

Friend, I know you feel the stirring in your heart. Maybe, for some of you, you've been feeling it for some time. You know God's calling you into something new and you're stuck because you think the dream is too big, or you're not equipped, or there's someone else who could do it better or maybe those around you have not been believing with you and praying you into this next season. You know you need to step out of the boat, but you're allowing your surroundings to hold you back.

Is your heart racing, even just a little as you read that? I feel like mine is too because I feel that so much for you. God's dreams for us are so much bigger than we could ever dream for ourselves. Why is that? It's because if they weren't we would go about our day thinking we don't need Him. We would lean on our own strength, our own knowledge or maybe the opinions of others, rather than constantly seeking Him.

Diving Deeper

How do you see God? Do you believe He sees you? Do you trust Him? Are you ready to be open to a deeper intimacy with Him?

I believe there are some of you who don't think God can use you. Somewhere along the line you started to believe that your past pain, hurts, or mistakes make it impossible for God to use you. Or maybe you've become content going through the motions. It's working, there are no risks involved. Do you ever wonder though, if you're missing out on something greater that God could want to bring you into or do in and through you?

You may believe that you'll never be like Peter, but the truth is, you will!

Posture of Prayer

Take a few moments in your journal to ask the Lord to show you areas of your life you have not entrusted to Him. Maybe you've felt stuck, and in your frustration, you've chosen to hold on to areas of your life that He wants you to release to Him. I want to encourage you to repent and release it all to Him. He can handle it. He wants to carry it for you. Begin to declare His promises over your life. Write down miracles and promises you've been waiting for and be sure to leave for to go back and date them when He answers them. He will answer them.

WEEK TWO

I am so excited for this week...

I loved being in the Word with you all last week and I'm so proud of you for committing to be vulnerable to what the Lord wants to do in your life throughout the next few weeks. Now that you have a week under your belt, week two is meant to solidify some concepts from week one and really dive into what it means to place our whole identity in who Jesus says we are. Last week we ended with the call to boldly step out onto the water and fully trust in all that Jesus has for us. It was a beautiful invitation that so often we believe is for others, but not for us.

I hope you spent some time giving Jesus your, "yes," to accept His invitation to step into the deeper and greater He has for your life. This week we will study some well-known Bible characters together who turn out to be a lot like us. We'll discuss what happens when we hide in our shame because we fear rejection. We're going to look at how we spend our time and does that time point to Jesus? It's the key to answering the question about where we are going to place the identities, we carry that weren't meant for us. Jesus paid a high price to give us a new identity in Him, but we live in a world where the enemy finds ways every day to tempt us to put it somewhere else.

This week will give us a chance to learn how to declare what God says about us and show us how to be intentional about intimacy with Jesus. As we spend time with Him at His feet, our love tank is filled! Finally, we will look at how spending time with Jesus is not just a one-time thing, it's a daily discipline. The enemy is always working to isolate us and steal the truth from our hearts about what God says we are. I'm excited to dive in together!

LIVE BOLDLY IN HIM,

Alisia

group discussion

Open with a time of worship together. There's a worship playlist in the appendix if you need some help picking out a song.

introduction

Who are you? When people introduce themselves to you, what do you want them to know about you? Maybe your name. Perhaps something about your family or your work. Those are typical responses. But, who do you tell yourself that you are – someone's daughter, someone's wife, someone's mother, someone's employee, someone's neighbor? Your identify in many ways is tied to who influences your life the most. Who's opinion matters the most to you?

come together

As we said last week, when we share our stories with others, we give them the opportunity to see God at work. Your story is being shaped, even in this moment, by being part of this group. In fact, few things can shape us more than community.

When we share our stories, we can encourage someone else, and learn. We experience the presence of God as He helps us be brave enough to reveal our thoughts and feelings.

Open your group with prayer. This should be a brief, simple prayer in which you invite God to be with you as you meet.

Begin your time together by using the following questions and activities to get people talking:

- Who do you think about the most? Why do you think about him or her?
- Who's praise lifts you up to cloud nine? Who's criticism ruins your day?

WEEK 2 | IDENTITY

watch video session 2
beknownbiblestudy.com/videos

group discussion

grow together

Read Psalm 139:17-19 (PT)

Every single moment you are thinking of me! How precious and wonderful to consider that you cherish me constantly in your every thought! O God, your desires toward me are more than the grains of sand on every shore!

- How do you feel about God always thinking about you? Is it reassuring or unnerving? Why?

Read Luke 10:38-41

- In what ways do you find it difficult to sit at Jesus' feet?
- How can we learn from Mary in this story about the importance of finding our identity in Jesus? Where you do you struggle with doing for Jesus instead of sitting with Jesus? Why do you think that is?

be together

In this section, talk about how you will apply the wisdom you've learned from the teaching and Bible study. Then think about practical steps you can take in the coming week to live out what you've learned.

- It's not always easy to see yourself the way Jesus sees you: beautiful, loved, worthy, created in His images, worthy, forgiven, strong… Which of these areas to you want to pray into with Jesus this week?
- Where are you going to make room in your day this week to spend time at Jesus' feet?

Prayer. Commit to personal prayer and daily connection with God. You may find it helpful to write your prayers in a journal.

Daily Homework. The Daily Homework provided in each session offers an opportunity for you to dive deeper with Jesus each week. I recommend spending time each day, walking through as much of the homework as you can. Freedom found in Jesus, first begins by our commitment to spend time with Him each day. To make space for Him in our lives.

Ask, "How can we pray for you this week?" Invite everyone to share, but don't force the issue. Be sure to write prayer requests in your prayer journal.

Close your meeting with prayer.

WEEK 2

daily study

DAY ONE

I remember playing hide and seek with my kids when they were really little. Eyes covered; slowly I would count to ten as the pitter-patter of little feet echoed in the space around me. 1...2...3...4... the sounds of giggles filled my ears as they searched for the perfect spot. Eventually, I could hear them settling in their hiding places. I would uncover my eyes and tell them I was coming to find them. Making loud noises, I walked around the house speaking in full volume, letting them know I was looking for them, but couldn't find them.

Each time I would get close, I could hear little giggles and see little fingers and toes sticking out from where they were hiding. But I would press on, wondering out loud where they were and if I would ever be able to find them. If I took long enough their patience would wane from the waiting and they would jump out from where they were hiding and exclaim, with a big smile, "here I am, Mama!" Even though I knew exactly where to find them the whole time, I would still act surprised when they jumped out, letting them know that I thought I was never going to find them. They would squeal with excitement and then ask if we could play again. Over and over we would play our game and they never seemed to tire of it.

HIDE AND SEEK

This is not far off from how we are as grown women. There are aspects of ourselves that we're willing to show those around us, to be vulnerable and present before God, but the rest of us we keep hidden. We fear putting it all out there opens us up to rejection, feeling inadequate and exposed. It's almost as if we're waiting for someone to find the hidden parts of us and affirm them. It's so much easier to be vulnerable when someone else makes the first move. Gosh, it can be so painful to think about taking those risks. Staying partially hidden always, especially in the digital age of social media, seems so much safer.

The Bible is filled with pages of those who played hide and seek with God, and with others. Yet, still, God sought them out, found them, healed them, blessed them, and as they began walking in that healing, they found freedom. Our unwillingness to do the work results in us missing out on the freedom that comes as a result. God has so many beautiful plans for your life; He doesn't want you to miss out on a single one by choosing to keep parts of yourself locked away. When we find Jesus, we discover what true intimacy looks like with Him. The closer we commune with Him, the less we worry about what others think, we're only concerned with His thoughts about us.

> When we find Jesus, we discover what true intimacy looks like with Him.

This week we're going to dive into what it looks like to live fully and completely confident in who Jesus says we are. There's no part of the earth you could move to that He wouldn't chase after you. After all, how could someone abandon their workmanship? Your creator, who named you, who calls you by name, desires for you to know Him as deeply as He knows you. It's so easy, with the heavenly divide, to think that we're an afterthought for God. He created us, dropped us here on earth, and moved on to the next thing. Oh, friend, this couldn't be further from the truth. As a result of this thinking, we play hide and seek with Jesus, appearing only when we need something from Him and doing our best to fly below the radar the rest of the time.

Are you willing to allow Him to turn areas of your life where you've been burdened by your past, your shame, and your insecurities into something beautiful? At what point are you willing to jump out and say, "Here I am Jesus!"?

Let's read Romans 8:38-39 together.

Please write the verses below.

Wow! There's a lot listed here that can and will try and separate us from the love of Jesus Christ. The enemy is always at work and He wins every time we believe that our Heavenly Father can't love us because..... you fill in the blank.

Let's go ahead and fill in that blank. What are some of the things you avoid talking to Jesus about?

Read Psalm 139:1-7 (NIV)

His word says that He _____ me and _____ me.

He knows when I _____ and when I _____. (vs. 1)

Before a word is even spoken from your mouth, He already knows what you're going to say. His desire for a relationship with us is so great that He wants us to stand firm on the knowledge that we were created to be in a relationship with Him, not sometimes, but all the time.

Read through those beautiful seven verses of Psalm 139 again. Which one of these is hard for you to digest that your creator could truly feel that way about you?

WEEK 2 | IDENTITY

Can you think of anyone else in the Bible who tried to hide from God to avoid shame, a mistake, a calling on their life? Let's look at a couple of examples together, shall we?

Genesis 3:8: _____

Jonah 1:1-3: _____

I Kings 19:1-4: _____

Write Jeremiah 23:24

As I sit here writing the Lord keeps bringing the woman who had been bleeding for 12 years (Luke 8:40-50) to mind. Bear with me. Neither Mark's account, nor Luke's shed light on how old the woman in this story is, but we can probably safely assume she's in her 20s. In the most pivotal, formative years of her life, when girls around her were becoming women, getting married, and carrying children, she was seeking doctor after doctor to find answers to a problem that made her an outcast in society. In those days, during that time of the month, women were considered ceremonially unclean and stayed home, avoiding people and the temple. If they even so much as brushed up against the clothing of another person, they would pass their uncleanliness onto them.

If there ever was a woman who tried to hide, it was this woman. She carried her shame, insecurities, and pain inwardly and outwardly. Even when she was in plain sight she was working overtime to not be seen. While at the same time, inside she was probably screaming out, "Here I am, come find me!" I imagine her desperation to be seen was what drove her that day she saw Jesus walking in the crowd. As she moved stealthily behind Him, this woman knew that all she needed was to graze her fingers on the hem of his garments and she would be healed. She became unaware of her shame. Can you imagine being that bold and that desperate that you would risk the anger of those around you, whom you touched, to get to Jesus? People who would be so angry that you had made them unclean.

Here we see this beautiful interaction between Jesus and this young woman. Jesus, in His goodness, could've allowed that woman to keep on with her life being half hidden from the world, but He didn't. He stopped, turned, and called out wanting to know who had touched Him. There was no doubt at that moment that Jesus was looking to find the woman. He wanted her to know that He saw her! He felt her pain, knew her loneliness, isolation, and shame, In that moment, He called out to her so that she would be seen, redeemed, and restored in front of the whole crowd, not just by Him.

He could've easily let the moment slide. Felt the power go out of Him, and being all-knowing, continued on His way, but He didn't. Don't you know Jesus wants to have the same encounter with you? He sees all the hidden parts of you and me and He loves us so much that He doesn't search for us quietly. No, He makes it known that He longs to be in relationship with us. He stands at the door and knocks, waiting for us to open it (Revelation 3:20).

Diving Deeper

Looking back on all we studied today, where do you feel convicted that you've been hiding from Jesus? How has that affected you from truly walking confidently in how your creator sees you? In what ways has your belief of how you think God sees you affected your willingness to trust him?

_____
_____
_____
_____
_____
_____

When your desire to encounter Jesus begins to outweigh the weight of the burdens you carry, He will be ready to meet you. He is ready to breathe new life into you. As you walk through the next five sections of this book:

WEEK 2 | IDENTITY

identity, purpose, gifts, season, and encountering Jesus, my prayer is that the women of the Bible and how they were seen, known, and used by God, will encourage you as you release any of those final hindrances you're holding onto so you can fully embrace all that He has for you. It may not look how you think it should. In fact, it probably won't look how you want it to but isn't that how God works? He never packages it up the way we think He should. No, He always does it so much better than we could ever imagine. I cannot wait to hear about how He shows up and speaks to you in your journey.

Posture of Prayer

To truly find freedom in Christ, we need to repent of the areas of our lives that we've kept hidden from Him. We read scripture that points to our creator knowing every thought and every action, even before we make them. There's nowhere we can hide from His love. Take a few moments and in your journal, ask for forgiveness for spaces of your life you've kept hidden from Him. Be honest with yourself and with Him about why you've lived that way. Then ask Him to help you let it all go so you can walk in freedom, knowing that He loves you and created you in his image.

DAY TWO

One conversation we've had a lot over the years in our home, with our children, is you are what you fill your mind with and the people you choose to spend time with. If you play video games all day then you risk becoming disconnected from the rest of the family, therefore isolating yourself. Or, if you choose to spend time with friends who feel it's ok to make fun of others, or put them down, even if you're not actively participating, you are still guilty of the behavior because you're not living differently. I tell them often they need to know who and whose they are and stand firm on that above all else. It's the same for us as adults. What we let fill our minds with becomes our identity. It becomes a focus, obsession, and a need to see that desire filled daily. For me, the struggle has always been social media. The need to curate a post, showcasing only the perfect corners of my life, then refresh constantly to see how many likes and comments I get.

For the last couple of years, the Lord has been actively breaking me of this. Sometimes now I go days between posting. I'm learning what parts of my life I will share publicly and which parts I keep to myself to honor my family. Sometimes they don't want to be on Instagram stories, or go live with me, or even want me to post about them. I realized that by putting my focus every day on what I can be posting and garnering attention to my little corner of the internet, I wasn't concerned with honoring myself, my family, or God. It was always about the followers, many of which don't even know me. The more I began spending my time in the presence of the Holy Spirit, the more it became about pleasing Him. If I'm being honest, it took some work to find

WEEK 2 | IDENTITY

breakthrough in this area because I had fully put my identity in what people online said about me and how they felt about me. Hear my heart, loves, I am not saying social media is bad, I'm just nudging you to keep your eyes on your creator, rather than who hits the like button on what you create.

WHAT YOU GIVE YOUR IDENTITY TO MATTERS

We don't always think about it but what we give the most amount of our energy and attention to is what drives everything we do. Some of those things in your life may seem trivial. Or maybe you don't feel you need victory over them. If you had brought up social media to me a couple of years ago, I would've smiled, nodded, and inwardly, adamantly disagreed with you that it had any hold on me. Maybe this isn't a crutch for you, maybe it's gossip, your children, your marriage, certain friendships, the enneagram. Yes, I went there! Anything you begin to use as an excuse for your behavior has become an idol in your life.

Read 2 Corinthians 5:17
Rewrite it in the margin, replacing 'anyone' with your name.

A big part of understanding our identity in Christ is knowing that when we surrender our lives to Him we become a new creation. What has bound us before, should no longer bind us. We have access to full and complete freedom in Christ!

Yesterday we talked about how easy it is for us to hide parts of ourselves from our creator. Even knowing that scripture says, there is nowhere we can go where He won't find us, our tendency is to believe what is out of sight is out of mind. Praise Jesus we're taking captive those thoughts and choosing to walk through the mud and mire so that God can refine us. He has so much planned for you, I can't wait to watch you find freedom and walk fully in all your gifts because you know who you are in Jesus.

Today we're going to look at what areas of our lives we've built altars to things and people that aren't God.

2 Corinthians 5:17

Write Isaiah 44:6

What is the definition of an 'idol'?

What is the definition of 'worship'?

An idol is a person or thing that is placed above God and given a position as a god in your life and worship is showing reverence and adoration. The Bible talks about worship as a way for us to come in full surrender to God, our creator, and honor Him. To give Him that position of Lordship over our lives. What you place above the one who created you, you allow to name you. And remember, sweet friend, only God gets to name you because He alone created you.

It's very easy for the things that we've allowed to become an idol in our lives to distract us. It is the result of someone giving you a false identity somewhere along the way. "You're not worthy." Well, my hundreds of thousands of followers on Instagram prove I am. "You won't amount to anything." But look at my corner office and seven-figure salary. "You're not loved." Well, I love my family to the point of exhaustion to prove I am loved.

What are some identities you've held on to? Who spoke those over you?

What does it mean to you to find your identity in Jesus?

To be known by someone, you have to be willing to step into a relationship with them. Not surface-level hellos and how's the weather where you are, but deep, intimate relationships. Where you don't hide partially behind couches waiting for someone to chase you down and pull you out from hiding, but the kind where you say, "here I am!" When we walk in relationship with Jesus in this manner, laying it all bare, wide open, being willing to pour out all the ickiness so He can fill it with all His goodness, there we discover how God feels about us. How deeply He loves and cares for us. When we enter that kind of relationship with our Lord, there we discover such intimacy and longing that we begin to see how He sees us. We begin to mold our identity around who Jesus says we are.

When was the last time you sat with the Lord and gave Him all the identities you've spoken over yourself or allowed others to speak over you? Friend, you are worthy to be known. Jeremiah 29:11 says, "For I know the plans I have for you, declares the Lord, plans for welfare and not for evil, to give you a future and a hope." God wouldn't create anything He doesn't deem worthy of using for His kingdom. Even if we find ourselves lost along the way, He will always be waiting close by, calling us back home to Him.

Who does Jesus say you are? Oh, sweet woman of God, let me tell you! I dare you to read them out loud to yourself, proclaiming each one over you. He says you are….

- Child of God *(John 1:12)*
- Forgiven *(Ephesians 1:7)*
- Saved by grace *(Ephesians 2:5)*
- Created in His image *(Genesis 1:27)*
- Free *(Romans 6:6)*
- Called me by name *(Isaiah 49:1-3)*
- Raise with Christ *(Colossians 3:1-3)*
- Child of God *(1 John 3:1)*
- Belong to God *(1 Corinthians 6:19-20)*
- Set Apart *(Jeremiah 1:5)*
- Healed *(1 Peter 2:24)*
- Created to Bear fruit *(John 15:5)*
- Strong *(Psalm 18:32)*
- Redeemed + Called *(Isaiah 43:1-2)*
- Rejoices over you *(Zephaniah 3:17)*
- God's Handiwork *(Ephesians 2:10)*
- Called Righteous *(Isaiah 42:6-7)*
- New Creation *(1 Corinthians 5:17)*
- Heirs of Christ *(Romans 8:16-17)*
- Friend of Jesus *(John 15:15)*
- Wonderfully Made *(Psalm 139:14)*
- Chosen *(1 Peter 2:9, Ephesians 1:4)*
- Confident *(1 John 4:17)*
- Blessed *(Ephesians 1:3)*
- Loved *(John 3:16)*
- Courageous *(Deuteronomy 31:6)*

Which one(s) are promises you're standing on right now?

Read Acts 9:1-19

What is the meaning of Saul's name? _____
(add it to appendix page 236)

Saul grew up in the Jewish faith. He was born to Jewish parents who also had Roman citizenship, which at that time, opened many doors in society. From a young age, he sat under the most knowledgeable Rabbi. He could recite the Torah front to back from memory from his formative years. He was a well-known Pharisee and persecutor of the Christian faith. The perfect example of how we can know scripture, but until we allow it to encounter our soul and transform us, it can be used as a tool to judge rather than to love.

It was on his way to Damascus that Saul encountered God. Instantly he knows who is speaking to him. Verse 4 says, "who are you, Lord." The Lord replies, "I am Jesus, who you are persecuting." Jesus doesn't ask Saul why he's persecuting His people or Christians or even the church, Jesus gets to the heart of it and points out that, in persecuting all those who believe, He is persecuting Jesus. I love how in one moment Saul goes from looking for Christians whom he can kill to immediate humility, surrendering to the move of the Holy Spirit that has overcome him, and asks Jesus, "what do you want me to do?"

How does God respond to Saul?

When Saul gets up to obediently go where God tells him, he discovers that he has been left blind. He's now completely dependent on the people traveling with him, but more importantly, on God, to take Saul where He wants him to go and protect him along the way. When Saul encounters Ananias, God uses him to perform a miracle, and Saul's vision is returned. Can we take a moment and give props to our man Ananias? I'm not so sure I would be rushing to meet the man who was known for killing Christians, let alone be willing to be part of his healing. That kind of humility and honor becomes the first example Saul receives post-transformation. Following receiving his sight Saul was baptized, filled with the spirit and he set out to preach the Word of God everywhere he went.

WEEK 2 | IDENTITY

There was one more transformation that happened, quite literally. Saul decided to forsake his Jewish name and replaced it with the Greek, Paul. Most likely because his ministry became focused on the saving of the Gentiles and they would resonate with his Greek name, Paul over his Hebrew one.

What does Paul mean? _____
(add it to appendix page 236)

Paul was devoted to God pre and post-conversion. It was his flesh and his self-righteousness that kept him from Jesus and salvation until he encountered Jesus on the road to Damascus. This man went from making his name great to be completely transformed and glorifying Jesus' name over his own. His mission became to give everyone the same opportunity to know Jesus the way he did. When we are made new by Jesus, we forsake our old selves, trading them in for a life of righteousness. Then in Acts 9:15 we literally see God give Paul a new name.

How does the Lord refer to Paul? _____

I believe the Lord wants to rename each of you. It may not be a physical name change, but He wants you to claim your name prophetically, standing boldly in who he said you are. I'll go first. My name, Alissa, hasn't changed, but I now know who God says I am. I once felt unworthy to be chosen or used by God, but now I know I am Alissa, noble, called to disciple women across nations and to shift atmospheres so they can experience transformation and healing in Jesus.

Now your turn....

"I, _____ [your name], _____ [meaning of your name], am called _____

_____

_____

_____

_____

Diving Deeper

We're going to end today with this. Will you do an activity with me? Tear a piece of paper out of the back of your journal and I want you to take a few quiet moments to pray and ask the Lord what old names you've been holding on to. Maybe look over the list on page XX and reflect on if you've struggled to stand confidently in its truth. Write old identities, tear them up and throw them away.

Can you feel the shift? I sense it so strongly as I write this. God is doing a work of transformation in your life. Yes, yours! He cares about every thought you speak over yourself or allow others to speak over you that doesn't come from His mouth. When we walk in the truth of knowing who Jesus says we are, we are no longer bound to the lies of this world and we get to find freedom!! Do you feel freer than you did when you opened your Bible at the beginning of our time together today?

Posture of Prayer

Now that you've torn up your old identities, take some time to journal and praise Jesus for His goodness, for His forgiveness, and, most importantly, that His greatest desire is for us to walk in full FREEDOM! When we know who Jesus says we are, it no longer matters what the world tries to place around our necks, we can stand on the truth. That person in your life does not get to name you! Thank your creator for the new names He's given you today.

(BE) KNOWN

DAY THREE

Yesterday I shared that for a long time I struggled with feeling chosen by God. There was always an excuse or a reason why I felt God could never use me. It was the mistakes I made in the past, decisions I had made where I knew I had disappointed God. It was watching other friends advance in their calling, making me reconsider if I had heard God correctly about my own. There were a lot of old wounds I had to work through and break free from to truly understand just how deep God's love is for me. To understand that all the things the Bible lists out, that's about how He feels about me. Every single one applied to me. Not one, not some, but all! And just like they apply to me, they apply to you. Your creator wants you to know how He created you, how He sees you and what He says about you. His thoughts about you outnumber the grains of sand. That thought alone leaves me with this heavey sense of awe and wonder. That God's thoughts about me, outnumber the grains of sand.

I don't know if you've ever visited the beach, but being in Southern California we live near the ocean. If I were to go and take a handful of sand and hold it between my fingers. Just allowing those grains of sand to slip through my fingers, I don't think I could even begin to

WEEK 2 | IDENTITY

list that many wonderful things about who God says I am. But praise Jesus, we can never take the place of our creator. What we can do is choose to stand confidently on all of the things He says we are. We are called, loved, chosen, and victorious. We are passionate, bold, and courageous..... And so one of the things I did in response to knowing that I struggled with coming into agreement the Lord says about me is I began to write declarations for those areas that I was struggling to know who I am and stand on who I am in Him.

DECLARING ALL THINGS NEW

Read 2 Corinthians 3:18.
Write it below.

I want us to do the same exercise. I'm going to share my personal declaration with you, but I want you to look at the list I shared with on day two (p. 63) of who God says you are. Now let's take a look at the one you feel you're struggling to accept about yourself, and now I want you to write a declaration, acknowledging that God has called you. He does love you, His love abounds for you, sweet friend. You are His chosen one! Whatever it is you let go of, in the space below, write out that declaration. Then I want to challenge you to write it on a sticky note or note card and put it somewhere you will see it every, single day.

Here's mine....

Chosen - **Ephesians 1:4**

I DECLARE that I have been created on purpose for a purpose. I have been equipped, anointed, and empowered. You, Lord, have planned big things for my life, far greater than I could ever dream for myself. I will pray bold prayers, filled with the expectation of dreams you plan to fulfill. Nothing is too difficult or impossible for you. You will begin giving me dreams and visions for my life. I will not be fearful or intimidated walking in the plans you have for me. For you have chosen me and you make no mistakes. I declare that I will walk in faith knowing that every dream big, small, hidden, or spoken will come to pass.

For he chose us in him before the creation of the world to be holy and blameless in his sight.

Ephesians 1:4

I struggle to accept that I am...

Now it's your turn...

_____
_____
_____
_____
_____
_____
_____
_____
_____
_____
_____

Today we're going to dive into a story about a woman in the Old Testament who spent time with God in the secret place. She knew who He said she was and she was used to bring wisdom, discernment, and victory to the nation of Israel.

Let's read Judges 4:3-24

I was part of a Bible study not too long ago and we studied the book of Judges. If you ever wanted a book that, at times, felt like a combination of Brave Heart and Game of Thrones, then study the book of Judges. Everyone is only interested in doing what they feel is right in their own eyes. Repeatedly the book of Judges says, "they did evil in the eyes of the Lord, they forgot about the Lord their God and they served the Baals and the Asherah's." (Judges 3:7). The only time we see peace is when God raises up a judge. Someone put in place to guide the Israelites into victories, help them resolve personal squabbles amongst themselves, and to point them back to God. When Deborah comes on the scene in Judges 4, she becomes the fourth judge, 20 years after the death of Shamgar, who killed 600 Philistines and saved Israel.

WEEK 2 | IDENTITY

After Shamgar's passing, the Israelites went right back to their old ways, again doing evil in the eyes of the Lord (Judges 4:1). Now they've found themselves enslaved to the King of Canaan whose army is mighty and takes delight in oppressing the Israelites. Once again they cry out to the Lord for deliverance. It was at that time that God raised up a woman named Deborah to lead the Israelites.

Let's pause for a moment and look up Deborahs' name:
_____ (add it to our chart on page 236)

Deborah was known as both a prophetess and a judge. Her name Deborah or D'vorah in Hebrew is translated as, "bee," which at first glance might not appear significant, but that couldn't be farther from the truth. Let's look at the beauty of Bees and how Deborah's name becomes so prophetically synonymous with how God uses her to bring the Israelites to victory against the King of Canaan.

1. Bees believe in community. They always travel together, build hives together, and gather pollen to come together as a community to make honey. Nothing they do is with selfish intention, but always with the forethought to take care of the larger group.

2. Bees all have a leader they follow. Similar to how we see the Israelites' desire throughout the Old Testament to submit to a king or leader and they follow Prophets to teach them.

3. A bee's sting can be painful, but the honey they produce is so sweet. Much like the Word of God, we read God's commands for our lives, and sometimes it's convicting because God is trying to bring us to healing and breakthrough. Other times it's a sweet confirmation and encouragement for the blessings that flow, the promises fulfilled for those who live a righteous life.

Before we dive into the beauty of Deborah's relationship with God and her confidence in who God says she was, I think it's important to talk about how she's referred to over and over as a prophetess, as well as a judge. I don't want to skip over the significance of her being known as both.

What is the definition of a prophet?

What do you know or understand about prophecy?

A Prophet or Prophetess is someone who hears from the Lord in a supernatural way, and therefore holds office over a group of people. Like Deborah, who was a Prophetess, but also a judge. She would hear from the Lord and sometimes that word would be meant for correction so the Israelites could live into the fullness of their relationship with God. They would come to her with their problems and she would have supernatural wisdom to bring resolution. Other examples of Prophets in the Bible would be Elijah, Jeremiah, and Isaiah. The Lord would give them a very specific word to correct the behavior of the Israelites and they would share it with the reigning King at that time.

The Spiritual gift of prophecy is most simply defined as a person who is dedicated to the reading of the Word of God and spending time in His presence and therefore is in tune with the Holy Spirit. They hear a word from the Lord for another person and they write it down, and share it with them. The gift, as Paul talks about in 1 Corinthians 14 is a Spiritual gift that you can desire and ask the Lord to receive. It's important to note that when operating in this gift, it should always be in alignment with scripture. It is not used to predict pregnancies or marriages, or borderline on new age thinking.

I want to acknowledge that, for some, the word prophecy can come off overwhelming or intimidating, so let's sit on it for a minute. I believe the Lord wants to have these hard conversations with us, to break off old thoughts and habits that keep us from fully knowing Him and hearing His voice.

How do you love to encourage your friends? Husband? Children?

WEEK 2 | IDENTITY

Write 1 Corinthians 14:3 below

The gift of prophecy is to edify, encourage and comfort those around you. Your friend is going through a hard time, ask the Holy Spirit for the words to build her up. It's asking the Holy Spirit to take a natural moment and make it supernatural! I was recently at a gala for a non-profit. My husband and I sat on the board for over seven years, even chairing the board for four of those. It was the first gala post-pandemic and many of us hadn't seen each other in three years. I was speaking to a couple, catching up, and they were sharing some health issues they had been healing from. Suddenly, I felt this strong urge to pray for them. So, right there, outside the entrance doors to the gala, I laid hands on the husband and wife and began to pray.

As I was praying the Lord gave me this beautiful picture of His presence in the room with them. I prayed for complete and total healing, but then I began to share with them that God was drawing them closer to Him and that He wanted them to picture their moments in the hospital and look for Him in the room. I went on to share how much Jesus loves them, He has never abandoned them, and even in those loneliest moments, to look for Him because He was there. They both began to weep. As I ended the prayer, they both shared with me that Jesus had been speaking to both of them that He will not abandon them and that He is always in the room and the car with them. Wherever they go, there He is too. Woah, right?! God is so good! He uses us to edify, encourage and uplift the body of Christ!

I have one more story to share with you all if that's ok. Several months ago I had been struggling with feeling like God's timing and mine were off. Maybe despite what I had perceived as an open door, I had heard wrong. I had felt so strongly that I was walking in obedience meeting with a book agent who

The gift of prophecy is to edify, encourage and comfort those around you.

I had been connected with. We had a great conversation, but, at the end of the call, I was asked for my book proposal. That should not be a "but" except I didn't have a completed book proposal. I was working to complete many areas of it and the truth was I had found myself stuck. I didn't know how long it would take to finish and edit it. Rather than leaving the meeting feeling excited, I let the enemy creep in and allow me to believe I would never complete it and therefore I wasn't meant to write the book.

Sunday morning I showed up to church early and a woman from the prayer team approached me. She and I were newer friends and I had not shared with her that I was in the process of writing my first book. She began to tell me that in her prayer time that morning, God had placed my name on her heart. He wanted her to tell me that He has called me to write! He told her I was working on some writing projects and I had been feeling discouraged about the timing of everything, but the Lord wanted her to tell me, He had not forgotten me, and to keep trusting in His timing. She not only saw books, plural, but also merchandise. God is good and He loves us so much!! He wants to use us to encourage one another!!

How do these stories shift how you view prophecy?

When was a time you shared a word of encouragement with someone and it felt as though the Lord was speaking through you?

Read 1 Thessalonians 5:11

Write it out below.

WEEK 2 | IDENTITY

Diving Deeper

In what ways are you edifying, encouraging, and comforting others around you? Is walking in these giftings difficult for you? Why or why not? Share a time the Lord used someone else to encourage you at a time when you needed it?

_____

_____

_____

_____

_____

_____

_____

_____

_____

_____

Deborah led the Israelites with both humility and boldness. This is how the Lord wants to teach us to lead. Before we can lead, we must first prioritize being in His presence. When we spend time with Him, we know how to hear His voice. That comes with making space for intimacy with Jesus. Giving Him our first and our best. Deborah had been appointed by God and she knew how to govern the people because she was in constant relationship with Him. We will talk more about this tomorrow!

Posture of Prayer

Take some time to journal and pray and ask the Lord if there's someone in your life who needs a word of encouragement. Ask Him to give you the words this person needs to hear from God. Write it down and then share it with them! If you're waiting on the Lord, take time to ask Him to begin to give you the blueprint for what's next. Remind Him that you trust Him and you love Him. Thank Him for giving you the gift of prophecy so you can use it to build up the body of Christ!

DAY FOUR

For most of my life, I was really good at going through the motions. Church on Sunday, Bible study on Monday, study homework during the week... wash, rinse, repeat. I never thought God would call me to lead women, write or even go into ministry. For a long time, I didn't even see how I led my family as a wife and mother who pointed to God for everything, as a ministry. I thought I would even score extra heavenly points because our children went to a Christian school during the week to help what they were learning in Sunday school take root. What I realized is that what takes root in our children's lives and solidifies their faith is how they see me spend time with Jesus. The greatest witness we can be to others is through our spiritual discipline.

Paul talks about running the race in 1 Corinthians 9. To train for a race you must have the discipline to train for the long haul, for the long-term prize, not short-term gain. That completely transformed how I saw my relationship with God. Not as something I had to strive for, but as someone I wanted to know. To truly know God, I needed to spend time in His presence. I began getting up early in

WEEK 2 | IDENTITY

the mornings to study my Bible and pray. I had a deep desire to pray and speak with Biblical authority to encourage those around me. To lift them up, edify them, and grow the body of Christ, beginning with my own home. It's been the greatest reward to have my kids wake up with me some mornings to read their Bibles, or before bedtime, tell me what God has been speaking to them. When we breathe in intimacy with Jesus, we breathe out His fragrance, and others can't help but want what we have, and the beauty is, we can share it. It wasn't intended for us to keep for ourselves.

HOW DO YOU FILL YOUR LOVE TANK?

Let's look at 1 Corinthians 9:24-27 (NKJV)

"Do you not know that _____ who run in a race _____ run, but _____ receives the prize? Run in such a way that you may _____ _____. And _____ who competes _____ _____ _____ is temperate in all things. Now they do it to obtain a perishable crown, but we for an _____ crown. Therefore I run thus: _____ _____ _____. Thus I fight: not as one who beats the air. But I _____ my body and bring it into subjection, lest, when I have preached to others, I myself should become disqualified."

I heard Beth Redman say once about this passage, "Spiritual discipline is your love tank," and it stuck with me. When we create spiritual disciplines, we become more like Jesus, and Jesus' greatest commandment was to love others, in truth and grace. How can we do that, if we don't know how to follow the greatest example of that, our Heavenly Father Himself?

What does your spiritual discipline look like in this season of your life? There are no wrong answers.

God desires for us to give Him our first fruits, the very best parts of us. For some that may look like praying first thing in the morning, while you're laying in bed before you pick up your phone. Maybe it's listening to worship music all day long, instead of your radio station of choice. I believe the Lord is saying, it's time to get ready, to get prepared. Jesus is coming back for His bride and He wants her to be ready. How do we get ready? We train! We dig deep in His Word. We practice praying with authority. We lead with love, grace, and generosity!

Let's look back at Judges 4 and pick back up where we left off yesterday with Deborah. She was both a judge and a prophetess, given this position of authority by God, not by man, which is why we don't see a lot of emphases placed on her husband or children. We know her position is ordained by God because the Israelites respect and honor her authority. They come to her with issues that need to be resolved, both big and small.

Read Judges 4:4-24 again to refresh your memory.

Where does Deborah hold court? _____

Take a moment to look up the Biblical significance of a palm tree. What did you find?

What might be the significance of Deborah holding court there?

Who does she send for? (vs. 6) _____

As a side note, Barack means, "thunderbolt," which suggests that he is called to be God's "flashing sword." He is also mentioned in the Hall of Faith, Hebrews 11:32 as someone, who by faith conquered kingdoms. I promise this is significant. Deborah was the first and only female judge over Israel and she was known for her prophetic abilities, remember we studied that yesterday. Where do your prophetic abilities come from? From studying God's word and being in His presence. That's where running the race for the heavenly prize that is imperishable comes in. The more we spend time in His presence, the more we learn His voice. How to hear it, discern it, and even be given words for others that will lead them to healing, breakthrough, and victory.

As a prophetess and a judge, appointed by God, we know that Deborah was a woman who chased after God. Judges 5, known as Deborah's song, points

WEEK 2 | IDENTITY

to her as a worshiping warrior. Where did she begin worshiping? In the secret place, in the stillness and the quiet. And because she worshiped in the secret place, the Lord prepared her for the calling and she was able to walk boldly and confidently in it because she knew how to hear God's voice. Her identity was placed in God, not in her position as a judge or prophet. She could've toted that she heard from God and therefore was more fit to judge over Israel. Instead, she referred to herself as the "mother of Israel," and a mother who always wants to guide and bring the best out of her children.

What does your secret place look like?

Who you are in the secret place is what pours out of you when you're around others. It's so easy to say in one breath that we just don't have the hours in the day to spend dedicated time with Jesus, but then we'll pull out our phones and scroll social media aimlessly or binge a Netflix series until all hours of the early morning. When was the last time you binged on God's word, or put on some worship music and sat for a whole song declaring God's goodness and singing the words over your life and your family? Deborah's worship and confidence to hear God's voice, led her to summon Barack and give him a word of victory from God.

Who you are in the secret place is what pours out of you when you're around others.

What was it? (4:6-7) _____

How does Barack respond?_____

Deborah tells him the Lord is commanding him to lead the Israelite army into battle against their enemies and He would bring them to victory. Barak responds that he will go as long as Deborah goes with him. Knowing she hears from God, and his lack of personal trust in God, Barack wants Deborah with him as he goes into battle because he believes the Lord will continue to reveal new strategies to her that will lead them to victory.

What does Deborah say in response to Barack saying he will only go if she goes with him?

Again we see Deborah operate in the prophetic. Her direct line to hearing from God is the result of her strong spiritual disciplines that she can hear His voice actively speaking to her and giving her wisdom in the moment. She tells Barack she will travel with him but because he refused to go without her, the honor that comes with the victory will not be his, but it will belong to a woman.

Share a time when you heard God speak to you in the moment? Was it for you or someone else?

The story wraps up with God causing Sisera's army to panic and Barak and the Israelite army defeat their entire army. Sisera, in the upset, ends up fleeing on foot. He finds himself in the tent of a woman named Jael, Heber the Kenite's wife. Knowing he thought he found himself a safe haven, he takes a drink she offers him and the opportunity to rest. Sisera lets his guard down when he accepts her invitation. He falls asleep and Jael drives a peg through his head with a hammer and delivers his dead body to Barak. Deborah's wisdom and discernment from God led the Israelite army to victory over the king of Canaan and Judges 5 ends saying, "the land had peace for forty years."

What Godly characteristics did you see in Deborah that are encouraging you to seek God in a deeper way in your own life?

Just as God led the Israelites into victory, God wants to help you find victories in areas of your life that have held you captive. I know we've walked through several exercises this week to complete cast off any chains that have held you back from spending time in God's presence, learning to hear His voice, and walking confidently in your identity in Christ, but if there's anything still lingering, I want to encourage you to take time journaling and praying through letting that go. Next week we're going to dive into our purpose and calling and we can't truly lean into that if we're walking without any hindrances.

Diving Deeper

Do you need to make some changes in your spiritual disciplines? Do you need to put some boundaries on other areas of your life so you can spend time with your creator who gave you life?

_____
_____
_____
_____

When we carve out time with our creator, we learn how to lean into His presence all day long, we breathe it in and breathe out His fragrance. Others begin to experience His fragrance flowing out of you and it encourages them to get into His presence for themselves. We can call others higher and into a deeper relationship with Jesus without words, but by simply exuding His presence and leaning into the prophetic wherever we go. Remember the Holy Spirit, living within you, gives you opportunities to use the prophetic to build up, encourage and edify the body of Christ. There's no greater gift.

Posture of Prayer

Take some time to journal and pray. Thank Him for his goodness and that He leads you to victory over the chains in your life that have kept you from hearing His voice. Then take a few minutes to ask Him if there's someone in your life He has a word of encouragement for. Does He have a word that will build up, encourage or give confirmation to someone you know? Remember, even if it doesn't make sense or resonate with you, the word is for them, so I encourage you to give them a call and share it with them. You can start by saying, "The Lord put you on my heart and I don't know if this resonates with you, but I wanted to share…" (Then share what the Lord put on your heart.)

(BE)KNOWN

DAY FIVE

I remember as a young adult I was invited to a conference my church at the time was putting on one weekend called, Heart Change. Having no idea what to expect from the weekend, I packed my bags in my dorm room, said goodbye to my college roommate, and hopped in my car to drive home for a couple of days. At the time I was attending a small, Christian college in Oregon and my parents were living in Salem. As I was driving the beautiful two-lane back roads, noticing the trees in bloom, I began talking to God about what to expect from the weekend. I had just gone through a pretty devastating breakup and my Dad had decided he wanted to separate from my Mom. I don't want to dishonor either one of my parents, this is their story to tell, I just remembered feeling so lost. As I'm writing this, God is showing me that we can know who we are at different points of our lives, but the enemy is always going to be trying to find ways to come in and steal that from us. For me, this was one of my moments.

In hindsight, I'm so thankful God knew that was coming and orchestrated that Heart Change conference, especially for me. When God wants our attention, He will find ways to weave our path back in line with His so we can encounter His presence. And, oh gosh, did

WEEK 2 | IDENTITY

I encounter His presence that weekend. At one point towards the end of the weekend, we were asked to sit in God's presence and ask Him to give us a vision of how He always wanted us to see Him. As I lay on the floor, yes the floor (haha), Jesus took me to this big open field of flowers. They were red, purple, orange, pink, and yellow. Not a tree in sight, just blue skies, puffy clouds, a breeze and an unforgettably beautiful fragrance. There in the middle of the field, I saw myself as a child. Jesus and I were running through the field together! Laughing and shouting with joy, we ran through the fields and Jesus picked flowers, made me a flower crown, and put me up on His shoulders. In that moment, all the weight I had been carrying left me, and I was left with peace and joy. Jesus has brought me back to that field many times over the years and every time I leave the same way, with awe and wonder of the magnificence of who He is and His love for me.

SITTING AT HIS FEET

Let's read together Luke 10:38-41

Before we get started today, let's take a minute to look up the meaning of Mary's name. What does her name mean? _____
(add to page 236)

This one might be one of my favorites. Beloved, what a beautiful picture that paints as we take a moment to imagine Mary sitting at Jesus' feet, absorbing every word He spoke. It's hard not to be a little envious that she tangibly knows what it feels like to be in Jesus' presence, hearing His voice, watching His mannerisms. What it must've been like to be there. It's moments like this that I'm so thankful that scripture reminds us of what Jesus gave us in place of His physical presence here on earth.

Write John 16:7

She had a sister called Mary, who sat at the Lord's feet listening to what he said.

Luke 10:39

He might've ascended to heaven, but He left us the greatest gift, the Holy Spirit, who lives in us, and walks with us, enabling us to feel His presence all the time. God is so good and He's a God who is all about the details. There isn't anything He hasn't put his fingerprints on, including you, my precious friend. I pray that as we begin day five together you've felt a huge weight lifted off of you and you're enjoying His presence surrounding you with His love, like a big, warm hug as you read His word.

It's funny how when you begin to prioritize being in His presence, sitting at His feet that there will be people in your life that will make comments like, "gosh it must be so nice to have time for that," or ask why you're trading out other things you used to be involved in, opting for time with Jesus. Maybe they won't understand God waking you up at 5:30 or 6 in the morning. Gosh, some mornings, I'm even surprised when the Lord, morning after morning, wakes me up that early. But I've never regretted missing those extra minutes of sleep. I can look back and clearly see all the things I would've missed out on by snoozing my alarm or rolling back over. In fact, I find that 7am comes all too fast and I'm not ready to leave His presence and go wake up my kids to start their day.

When we know the power and satisfaction that comes from being in His presence, we begin to feel like we can never get enough. Thank you, Jesus!!

Read Luke 10:42
Write it below.

Mary and Martha, sisters of Lazarus, lived in a village about two miles outside of Jerusalem. The village was called Bethany. Both women were known for their hospitality and love for Jesus and the disciples. Jesus has made His way to their village, passing through after leaving Jerusalem. Martha invited Jesus and his disciples to her home to prepare a meal for them. Immediately, Martha begins the preparations for the meal, but it becomes a point of contention between the two sisters.

What is Mary doing? (vs 29) _____

Mary is found sitting at Jesus' feet. What comes across as so evident in this passage is that both women loved Jesus wholeheartedly and had a deep desire to be in His presence. It's how they go about it that is different. In those days it would be completely uncommon for a woman to be allowed to sit at the feet of a Rabbi and learn. That honor was reserved for men. What we see time and time again throughout Jesus' time on earth is how He constantly shifts that narrative and honors women as disciples, preachers, and teachers, and often invites them into the same company as men. Jesus approaches children the same way.

The difference we see between how these two women approach Jesus' presence is that Martha sees it as a luxury. Once the work is done, she will sit at Jesus' feet and enjoy time with Him, whereas Mary sees it as a priority. I don't say this to shame anyone, in fact, I've spent a lot of my life as a "Martha." Here I am Lord, do you see all I am doing for you? Over the years the Lord has convicted my heart. Not to scold me for "doing," but to remind me that serving the Kingdom must first start with a deep desire to sit and be present in His presence.

I'm sure Martha spent much of her preparation time trying to get Mary's attention, working overtime to make eye contact, to give her the hand signals so she would know she was needed. Until finally, we see Martha throw her hands up in exasperation and complain to Jesus.

Do you think Jesus knew Martha was getting to the tipping point? Why do you think He allowed her to reach that point?

Jesus knew Martha was a beautiful host, but He also knew time with Him was precious. Martha was serving in a way that assumed Jesus would always be here on earth, available to spend time with her. Jesus knew His time was limited and He wanted to help Martha "prepare" or be ready in a different way. Even when she loses her patience, Jesus replies, "Martha, Martha." Not in a condescending way, but in a familiar, loving way. In a way that showed her He saw her, He saw all the preparations she was making for the meal, but what He really wanted, more than food was to enjoy her company.

Jesus was trying to teach Martha that He is the bread of life. What He has to give her will sustain her, nourish her and satisfy her soul so much more than her bread could. He was offering that to her and to everyone else who was visiting with Him in their home that day. We see this beautiful moment of Jesus ministering right to the heart of Martha, affirming her identity (serving/doing), but also inviting her into a moment to see how else He saw her beyond her servant's heart. That is so beautiful.

We never want to lose the awe and wonder of sitting in God's presence. That's why I love Mary so much in this passage. She never picks a fight with her sister, she never pulls her from preparations and scolds her for missing an opportunity to sit at Jesus' feet. She's so caught up in the awe of His presence, that it becomes her sole focus. Whatever she gets from Jesus in her time with Him sustains her so much that we see two other interactions with Jesus where her first response is to run to His feet.

Read John 11:32-33

"When Mary finally found Jesus outside the village, she _____ at his feet in tears and said, "Lord, if only you had been here, my brother would not have died." When Jesus looked at Mary and saw her weeping ____ _____ _____, and all her friends who were with her grieving, he shuddered with emotion and was ____ _____ with tenderness and compassion."

Read John 12:1-3

What brings Mary back to Jesus' feet in this passage?

Like Mary, do you look for moments to sit at Jesus' feet? Do you find God in the secret place like Deborah? These women are a beautiful example of how the Holy Spirit moved in and through us when we prioritize spending time with Jesus. It would be difficult to say we truly know or are known by our friends if we don't spend intentional time with them, why would we think we know our creator, without doing the same? My prayer is that this week has encouraged you to seek out the presence of God every day. What that spiritual discipline looks like for you is going to be different than what it looks like for me and that is ok! Spending time with Jesus should never feel like a chore, a competition, or a check the box. It will always leave you fulfilled, yet wanting more.

WEEK 2 | IDENTITY

Diving Deeper

When was a time you encountered the Holy Spirit, sitting in His presence, and didn't want to leave? What do your spiritual disciplines look like? Is the Lord challenging you through this study to make some changes?

_____

_____

_____

_____

I don't want to miss out on a single moment to spend time in the Lord's presence and give Him the first and last fruits of my day. We will only regret the things we missed out on or didn't do. Just as Jesus knows how many hairs are on your head and His thoughts about us outnumber the grains of sand (Psalm 139), how will we ever know what those thoughts are if we don't sit at His feet? One of the things that has stayed with me as I was studying for this week is that we see three interactions between Mary and Jesus in the Bible. Each one always points to Mary being at Jesus' feet. She sat at His feet to learn, she threw herself at His feet when her brother died and she cried and poured perfume and her tears, washing His feet in His last days. It really convicted me. Do I do that? No matter what is going on in my life, is my first desire to seek Him? If we want to rediscover our identity in Jesus and find that awe and wonder that comes with knowing Jesus intimately, we have to spend time at His feet.

> If we want to rediscover our identity in Jesus and find that awe and wonder that comes with knowing Jesus intimately, we have to spend time at His feet.

Posture of Prayer

Spend some time journaling and praying. I want to challenge you to change your posture as you pray and journal today. Put on some worship music, find your way to your knees and begin asking Jesus to show you what it felt like for Mary to sit at His feet. Ask Him to give you extra moments in your day to spend time in His presence. As He begins to speak to you, write it down in your journal. Maybe He will give you a vision, like the one He gave me of us running through a flower field, or maybe He will pour over you words of affirmation you've been longing to hear. Write it down so you can always go back and reread it.

WEEK THREE

I'm so excited for what God is going to do this week as we continue digging into His Word together!

Did you know that God has woven passions, gifts, and callings into your life? In fact, He was already doing so from the time you were a little girl. If you think about it, you might be able to remember the moment when you first noticed your heart to serve, to help others, to teach, or to lead. We're going to talk a lot about that this week as we dive into the word God has for us.

We're also going to look at times in the Bible when people had to wait for their passions and promises to come to fruition. God might have declared the promise, but so often there was a season of waiting that followed. We can learn a lot from these men and women of God about how to wait and how we can let God carry us even when our dreams feel delayed. Maybe you feel as though you've delayed your own dreams because of decisions you've made in your life, but that's the beauty of redemption. God wastes nothing! There's no part of your testimony that won't bring healing and transformation for others. We see this when Jesus goes out of His way to Samaria on His way to Galilee. It was there a Samaritan woman's passions and gifts were activated when Jesus made a point of encountering her at the well. She shows us how, with His help, we can leave our past in the past. The beauty of this week comes in the form of encouragement as we study about how each and every one of us is uniquely gifted because we are uniquely known! My prayer is that as we jump into this week, you find yourself encouraged and excited to see how God is going to fulfill those promises in your life.

LIVE BOLDLY IN HIM,

group discussion

Open with a time of worship together. There's a worship playlist in the appendix if you need some help picking out a song.

introduction

Do you know that God has designed a purpose specifically for you? It can be so each to feel as though He doesn't see you or know the passions He's laid on your heart. When was the last time you took some time to share with Him the desires of your heart? It can be really easy to feel as though everyone else around you is walking in their calling and you're stuck in the same cycle of diaper changing, working 40 hours a week, doing laundry, long carpool lines. But the Lord has beautiful and wonderful plans for your life. They begin in your home, with the Spiritual foundation and legacy you're laying and they extend into your workplace and passions. Have you ever thought about God wanting to share in your passions with you?

come together

Open your group with prayer. This should be a brief, simple prayer in which you invite God to be with you as you meet.

Sharing personal stories builds deeper connections among group members. Begin your time together by using the following questions and activities to get people talking.

- What's something you are a big fan of?
- What's one thing in your house that you just hate to clean?

watch video session 3

beknownbiblestudy.com/videos

group discussion

grow together

Read Psalm 34:8

Taste and see that the Lord is good; Blessed is the man [and woman] who trusts in Him.

Read 1 Samuel 12:16

Now then, stand still and see this great thing the Lord is about to do before your eyes.

Have women in your group take turns reading John 4:1-26

- What did the woman at the well need?
- What did the woman at the well receive from Jesus?
- Your story might be very different from the woman at the well, but how does Jesus' regard for her make you feel?

be together

I God wants you to be part of His Kingdom—to weave your story into His. That will mean change. It will require you to go His way rather than your own. This won't happen overnight, but it should happen steadily. By making small, simple choices, we can begin to change our direction. The Holy Spirit helps us along the way, by giving us gifts to serve the body, offering us insights into Scripture, and challenging us to love not only those around us but those far from God.

In this section, talk about how you will apply the wisdom you've learned in this session.

- How have you witnessed the greatness of God in your life? Tell the group.
- What do you need from Jesus?
- How do you feel about Jesus' ability and willingness to meet your need?
- Have you asked Jesus to meet your need? Why or why not?
- What steps will you take this week to grow in your relationship with God? The daily homework is a great way to connect with God each day and grow a deeper relationship with Him.

Ask, "How can we pray for you this week?" Be sure to write prayer requests in your prayer journal. If you don't have one, be sure to check out the one in our toolbox.

Close your meeting with prayer.

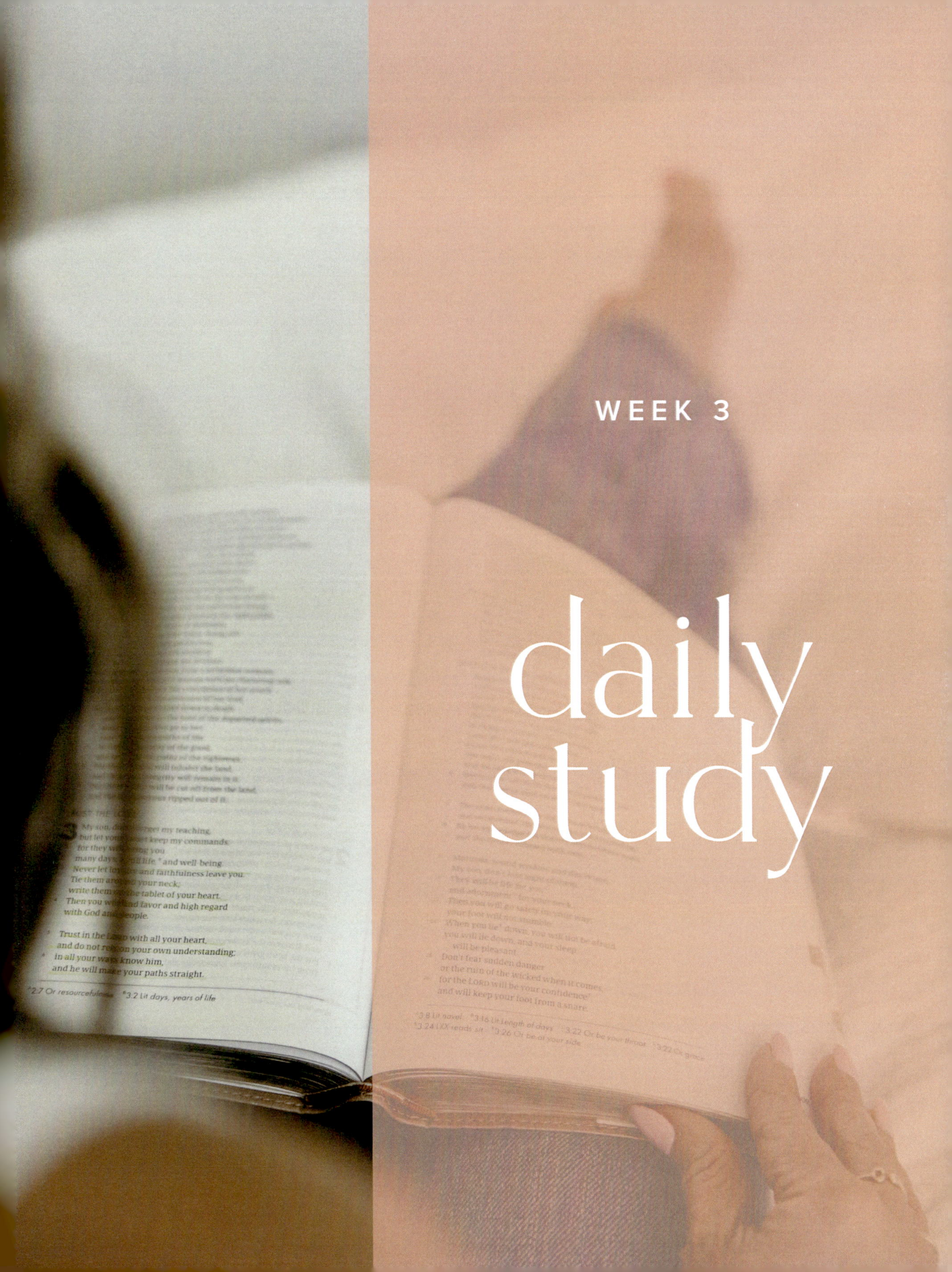

WEEK 3

daily study

DAY ONE

I had the most incredible fifth grade teacher. Mrs. Thompson changed my life in the best way possible. Because of her, I wanted to become a teacher. The Lord used her that year to bring out passions and desires in me I didn't even know existed. While she was strict, she was also kind — but what I loved most about her is that every child in her class felt seen. I have vivid memories of her building up and encouraging our class collectively and individually. Every day I went home believing I could achieve even the most impossible tasks. I only had her for one year, but who she was and the way she loved her students has stuck with me to this day. That was over 30 years ago. Our family moved to Malaysia a year later and I never made it back to tell her how much she meant to me.

I thought about Mrs. Thompson a lot over my junior high and high school years. Then one afternoon my junior year of high school, in a whole other country, there she was walking down the hallway. She was visiting for teacher training and found out I was a student there. She had been looking for me to say hello. All those years later and she remembered me as well! I was able to sit with her and share how much she meant to me and that because of her I was going to college to become a teacher. My heart was to help kids feel seen and known, and show them they could achieve anything they set their minds to. I wanted to show God's love to children in hopes they would carry His goodness in their hearts forever. What a beautiful moment it was!! God is so good and I was so grateful to be able to share that moment with a teacher who had impacted my life. I still wonder about her to this day, where she retired, and what she's doing now.

WEEK 3 | PASSION

GOD WOVEN PASSIONS

What passion(s) did God put on your heart at a young age?

What does that look like today?

When I left Malaysia at 18 years old, I moved to Oregon to attend a small, Christian college. For three years I was part of their elementary education credential program. In the fall of 2001, I found myself worn out by the constant rain and dreary weather and traded clouds for sunshine. I transferred to a university in Southern California to finish school here. I graduated with a degree, received my credential, and Masters degree in Education. I taught in several grades during my student teaching years, but my first job was in a middle school classroom teaching English to 6th-8th graders. I was terrified!! Most of them were taller than me for one! At 24, I felt like we were all so close in age, would I even be able to establish any control of the class to teach these brilliant young minds? And gosh, they were amazing kids! I truly believe those years were God's gift to me. My kids are both teenagers and I will stand by these being some of my favorite years with them.

1 Samuel 12:16

Read 1 Samuel 12:16
Write it out in the margin.

Doesn't this verse encourage you so much?! It has carried me through the last three years, since the moment the Lord asked me to begin laying down my business to serve Him in a new way. When He gave me the title and chapters for my book in April of 2019, I would never have guessed the journey of refinement He would take me on over the next couple of years. To be honest, I struggled a lot during those years of waiting on the Lord for what my next season was going to look like. The wilderness felt long, and the refinement process was hard, but looking back I can see the manna the Lord fed me daily during the last few years.

See, it's easy to think that when God shifts us from one job or calling to another, we've somehow done something wrong. We begin to question our calling. But if we were to take a moment to look back, we would see a God-woven pattern that has taken us from when God first ignited that passion in us, to today! I hope you saw that connection when you responded to those first questions from today. God wants you to know that the gifts He has given you don't change. The purpose in which He calls you to use them might change throughout the different seasons of your life. To get to that point, we need to be willing to STOP and work on ourselves from the inside out.

Last week we focused on the importance of being in God's presence. When we get into His presence, it's there that He begins to ignite our passion for our calling. They are interwoven. They cannot exist apart from each other. You can't run in your calling without being in His Word and resting in His presence to allow Him to be the fuel that keeps your passions ignited.

Let's read Proverbs 16:3 together (NIV).

"Commit to the Lord _____ you do and He _____ _____ your _____."

When was the last time you re-committed your plans to the Lord? Surrendered them as the desires of your heart and gave them back to the Lord so that He could steer you in the direction you should go? God has plans to prosper us, to give us a hope and a future (Jeremiah 29:11). He's not out to harm us or throw a wrench in our plans. Who do you think gave you the blueprint for that passion, to begin with? He did! When we refuse to give our plans and our desires to Jesus with the knowledge that He first planted those thoughts in our hearts, we are telling God we don't trust Him to fulfill those plans. We want Him to give us all the details, but then we don't trust that He will orchestrate them. It would be like going to an amusement park, riding a roller coaster a couple of times, and then thinking you can take over running the ride as the operator.

Where, in your life, have you been trying to sit in the driver's seat and move Jesus to the passenger side?

Why do you think that is?

Trusting God in all things is so much easier said than done. We feel the tension of the fine balance between allowing God to have complete control and wanting to run ahead of Him, even just a little bit. There are five key things I believe God wants us to meditate on before we dive into the rest of this week, allowing Him to reignite our passions in a new way.

1. Following God doesn't mean He's going to lay it all out for you at once. If God showed us His entire plan for our lives all at once, would we struggle to live by faith? In our selfish nature, we would take the reins and try to control every aspect of our lives. We like to barter with God that if we just knew the direction of our lives, we would have peace. Is there truth to that though? Would you live in peace if you knew what God's 50-year plan for your life looked like, or would you be constantly striving to make it all happen faster than God planned it?

2. God's plan is not always our plan. It's better! This one is just as convicting for me as it might be for you. It was heartbreaking for me to accept; especially learning at a young age that the plan I thought I had wasn't the plan God had for me. I will tell you with full confidence that I wouldn't go back and change the road that brought me here. Even though there are moments of heartbreak, frustration, and wondering if the Lord understood what I was going through.

3. While the gifts that God gave us don't change, how He chooses to use them for His kingdom impact can. When I got my teaching credential, I always saw myself in a classroom molding young minds for the rest of my life. Today, I know with confidence that teaching is one of my gifts, but over the last 10 years, God has given me the honor of teaching young minds and women alike.

4. If you can't let go, you can't truly let God. You have got to be willing to drop your bags at the door and surrender to God before He can truly use you in the way He so desperately desires. Trust is hard, but it can be so rewarding when we give control over to our Heavenly Father.

5. Your past does not define God's plan for your future. He does not look at your mistakes and label you as damaged goods. You may think that you're not worthy of the gifts He's given you, but He wants you to lean into Him so He can bring out those passions He has put inside of you. He wants that for you friend, please don't let your pride get in the way of all that God can do through your life.

Which one of these are you struggling with today?

For I know the plans I have for you," declares the Lord, "plans to prosper you and not to harm you, plans to give you hope and a future.
Jeremiah 29:11

I have written Jeremiah 29:11 in the margin, before we close out today, I want you to write this verse out, but I want you to personalize it.

"For I know the plans I have for you _____ [insert your name]," declares the Lord, "plans to prosper you, _____ [your name] and not to harm you, plans to give you hope and a future."

Scripture is alive and God-breathed. The promises that fill the pages are for each and every one of us. If you're struggling to hold onto them I would encourage you to put your name in scripture! Those promises are not just for then, they are for now, for you and me. Praise Jesus!!

Diving Deeper

In what ways have you been struggling in finding your purpose this season? Was there a major event/shift in your life that happened to cause you to feel that way? What answers are you looking for from the Lord?

_____
_____
_____
_____
_____

WEEK 3 | PASSION

Isn't the waiting game so hard? If we were sitting together I would give you the biggest hug and tell you I've been there and there's no doubt in my mind God has destined you for great things. If you stop and wait and seek Him, He will show you how He will fulfill his purpose in your life. Psalms 57:2 says, "I cry out to God Most High, to God who will fulfill his purpose for me." Friends, try as you might, you can't argue with what's written in plain black and white. God will fulfill His purpose in you.

Posture of Prayer

Grab your prayer journal and take some time to share with the Lord how you're feeling. If you feel you're walking fully in your passion or calling, thank the Lord for His goodness and ask for continued wisdom. If you feel like you're in a place where you're seeking the blueprints from the Lord for what's next, spend time asking the Creator for discernment.

I cry out to God Most High, to God who will fulfill his purpose for me.
Psalm 57:2

(BE) KNOWN

DAY TWO

Waiting is so hard when you're a Type A, driver personality. Let's be real, it's hard no matter what your personality type is. There's nothing glamorous about being in a season of waiting. I keep thinking of how the Israelites felt, wandering the wilderness for 40 years. Promised Land is in sight, yet just out of reach. I remember having coffee with a friend a couple of years back and was sharing with her that I felt like God was moving me into a season of transition. He was shifting me out of the being CEO of my company and had put a desire in my heart to write a book. She peppered me excitedly with questions about the book, yet I found myself without answers. None. God hadn't given me that part of His plan yet. In the back of my mind, I'd always thought I would write a cookbook that incorporated recipes from my family heritage and my world travels. A travel guide and cookbook all in one. Yet, in that moment all I felt prompted to say is that I knew I was supposed to write a book. I had no idea about what, when, or how it would happen and felt the Lord tell me to wait for Him for the timing.

I walked away from our time thinking how she must've thought I was crazy! Honestly, I'm laughing as I type this thinking back to that sunny day outside the coffee

WEEK 3 | PASSION

shop. Being an entrepreneur and go-getter, similar to myself, I loved that she was pushing me to reach for my goals. Yet I couldn't help feeling a little frustrated that God had instilled a new passion within me, but I had no idea how it was going to be achieved because I didn't fully understand what it was. Now here I am; obediently putting the words the Lord has given me to paper. If you didn't think God had a sense of humor, this Bible study and my book can serve as proof. God calls us to things we never expect, and oftentimes His dreams for us are so much larger than our dreams for ourselves.

HIS DREAMS ARE LARGER

We often believe the lie that we will find our purpose in our busyness. Meetings, multiple incomes, play dates, sports, school, carpool pick-ups, and multiple Bible studies. None of which are bad, but if you're searching for meaning in those things, you won't find it there. The only place you will find your purpose is by spending time in the presence of your Creator. When we get caught up in the "doing" we miss out on opportunities to be the sweet aroma of Jesus in everyday moments of our lives.

What would change in your life if you asked God to slow down your day and make room for time for Him to meet you?

Friend, just like you won't find your identity, let me tell you right now, you will not find your purpose in busyness either. Has your life become like a Rolodex where you sift through the cards to grab what comes next? Maybe life feels like a game of Wheel of Fortune where you're constantly spinning, but wondering if you're going anywhere. When priorities become centered around movement: get up, get ready, husband, kids, work, school, drop offs and pickups, sports, etc, we often feel lost in our busyness and our sense of purpose becomes lost in the shuffle.

What would it look like if you just stood still? Slowed down. Took a break. Took the time to meditate on Jesus with slow, long deep breaths and worship music playing. You might tell me this is easier said than done, but my response would be, if you've lost the joy of who you are and you feel as though you're moving through life to serve everyone else's purpose, but you are lost, you need this, my friend. Even Jesus knew who He was to His Father and because of this was able to turn the world upside down in just three short years. Let's take a look at how Jesus' ministry began. It wasn't in a palace. There was no one crowning Him king. No, it was in the desert.

Let's read Matthew 3:16 - 4: 11

Jesus has just been (3:16) _____

Right after He's baptized what happens? (3:16-17) _____

The sky immediately opens up and Jesus is identified by His Father. "This is my Son, whom I love; with Him I'm well pleased." Jesus hadn't even stepped into His calling and God was affirming who He was, reminding Jesus He is loved and that God is pleased with Him. Did you know that God speaks those same words over you? Even if you feel as though you haven't stepped into your calling yet, or maybe you're smack dab in the middle of it, He loves you, He calls you by name and He's so pleased with you. Do you believe that?

What happens directly after the Spirit of God ascends on Jesus? (4:1)

When I first read this I was awestruck? Jesus has just had this precious moment with His Father, the Spirit falls on Him, tender like a dove, yet bold like lightning, and straight into 40 days of fasting, followed by the enemies tempting He goes. It's not much different than our lives. The second you begin to step into your calling, bam, the enemy starts finding ways to sneak in and cause problems. He will try to make you second guess yourself and your identity. Which then makes you question your calling. Before you know it, you've given up before you've started, or maybe mid-way through. In this passage, we're given the blueprint for how to combat the enemy when this happens so we can walk confidently knowing that we are called by name, we are loved and He is pleased with us. How do we do this? Let's look at the passage together.

After forty days and forty nights of fasting, the devil comes to Jesus and tempts Him in three ways (Matthew 4).

As soon as Jesus was baptized, he went up out of the water. At that moment heaven was opened, and he saw the Spirit of God descending like a dove and alighting on him. And a voice from heaven said, "This is my Son, whom I love; with him I am well pleased."

Matthew 3:16-17

Matthew 4:3 (NIV)

"If you are the Son of God, _____ these stones to become _____."

Satan is saying to Jesus that He doesn't need God, after all, isn't He God too? If so, show His power, and turn the stones into bread so He can eat. Just like in the garden (Genesis 3). Once again the enemy is lurking and trying to tempt Jesus to act outside of His Father. Immediately Jesus shoots back and says, "Man does not live by bread alone, but by every word that comes from the mouth of God." When we know God's Word, we can stand on His truth. When the enemy comes prowling with his lies, we know how to stand strong in the trial because we can proclaim God's promises with our mouths. When we speak, demons tremble.

How often do you spend time in God's Word, memorizing scripture so you can combat the enemy's lies?

Matthew 4:6 (NIV)

"If you are the Son of God," he said, "_____ yourself down. For it is written: He will command his _____ concerning you. They will lift you up in their hands, so you will not strike your foot against a stone."

Satan isn't questioning Jesus's divine nature or His calling, he's trying to tempt Him to use His powers selfishly for His own good. Our callings should never exist for selfish gain, but always for the betterment of others. Satan says, "go ahead and throw yourself off this mountain and command your angels to save your life to prove you are who you say you are." Jesus replies again with the truth of the Word of God. "Do not put the Lord your God to the test." He's saying, I will not be tempted by you, but do not test God because you may not like the outcome. Isn't this like the enemy when it comes to our calling? God gave it to you, but Satan wants you to question if you need Him to achieve it?

When is a time God has blessed your family and/or business and you've told God you'd take it from here and try to do things in your own strength? What happened?

Matthew 4:9 (NIV)

"All this _____ will _____ you," he said, "_____ you will _____ down and _____ me."

Again, a third time the enemy is trying to tempt Jesus by making Him believe that everything He sees from the top of that mountain isn't already His. The enemy hasn't forgotten who created it, he just likes to get in there and make us think that the glory will be bigger, grander, and richer if he's the one who gives it to us. It's at this point we see Jesus become fed up and speak scripture one final time. "Worship the Lord your God, and serve Him only." The glory belongs to the one who created you. It's He who has the blueprints for your life, who won't lead you astray, who won't make you question who you are and why you serve Him.

What other gods have you been serving in hopes that they will help you get ahead in your calling? (Gossip, social media, networking)

Choosing your plan for your life over God's is only delaying God's best for you. It's giving voice to your self and telling God that He might've created you in His image, but that doesn't mean He knows what's best for your life. It's arrogant and prideful and leaves no room for the Holy Spirit to work in and through you. In Acts 2, the Word talks about 120 people who gathered in the upper room to pray as they waited on the Holy Spirit. Over 500 people saw Jesus after He rose from the dead. Only a handful of them obediently went where they knew they could find His presence to let Him lead what would be the next season of their lives.

WEEK 3 | PASSION

Are you willing to take a look at areas where your pride has kept you from seeing what God can do? I wish I was just speaking to you right now, but I'm 100% speaking to myself as well. We need to let the Lord's convictions lead us. We need to be Jesus in our "desert" moments and the mountaintop ones where we feel things are going great. Where in your life do you need to tell the enemy to take a hike?

Diving Deeper

Do you need to take some time to rededicate your life and your purpose back to God? Have you found yourself walking on your own path because you don't think you need Jesus to walk fully in your calling? Or maybe He's moving too slow, so you've taken matters into your own hands, do you need to take a moment and repent for not trusting His timing?

_____
_____
_____
_____
_____
_____

God wants to walk with us not in front or behind us. When it feels like the struggles are too much to bear, that's when He picks us up and carries us. Those are the moments when we need to know His Word, so we can combat the enemy's lies with His truth, His promises, and His love for us. There is nowhere you can go where He will not follow (Matthew 18:12). Let Him put His fingerprints all over the blueprints of your calling and watch and see what He can do for you.

Posture of Prayer

Grab your prayer journal and take some time to pray and invite the Lord back into every area of your life. Surrender areas you haven't trusted Him and ask Him to help you walk with Him. Ask Him to renew your love for spending time with Him in His presence.

DAY THREE

I was engaged at 19 years old, right around the time my parents' marriage was ending. He was older and had a stable job. I was a freshman in college. Within a few months of dating, he proposed to me in front of my family and I said yes. Instead of being one of the happiest moments in my life, it was one of those moments I'll never forget because I remember feeling like I was watching it happen as a spectator in the room rather than as a participant. Still, I threw myself excitedly into wedding planning. This was my plan after all. One I had held onto since I was a small girl. Go to college, get my degree, get married and start a family. I was so sure I needed to start young so I had plenty of time to have babies before I was 30. My college friends raised red flags to me that I ignored. I brushed them off as him just being older than us and being out of college, therefore, lacking patience with the rush of the college scene. I didn't want to see what was right in front of me.

My wake-up call came a few weeks later when I received a call from an acquaintance who knew my fiancée and me. In one sentence he shattered my whole world when proceeded to tell me he had seen my fiancée with *another woman. Shocked and frustrated, ugly tears streaming down my face I wondered where I had gone wrong. Confronting him, he made it all about my lack of trust while refusing to deny that he had been unfaithful. Red flag, ladies. I know that now. I told him I needed time and drove home to see my mom. I broke down, shared what had happened, and asked her to hold onto the ring and keep it safe till I knew what I was going to do. That was the last time I had that ring on my finger. Looking back, I don't know why I hesitated to make a clean break. Maybe because it felt as though my purpose was slipping through my fingertips. Maybe I had allowed identities I had adopted to cause me to question if I deserved better. Everything I thought I had wanted went up in smoke. In the end, I called off our engagement and gave him back his ring.*

LEAVE IT AT THE WELL

Today I'm so excited to spend some time with one of my favorite women in the Bible. I know, I will say that about all of them, but God included so many beautiful women in the Bible, who encountered Jesus in ways that dynamically changed their lives. Today we're going to join Jesus by a well, known as Jacob's Well, located in Samaria. Where a woman arrived one way and left completely changed after her interaction with Jesus. We might not know her name, but I wonder if Jesus doesn't prompt John to include that on purpose. This nameless woman could be any one of us.

Let's read John 4:1-26 together.

Where do you find yourself identifying with the woman at the well?

We don't know the name of the woman at the well that Jesus encounters. We can't add the meaning of her name to our chart, but I do want to take a few minutes to understand why this whole interaction is so Jesus. Remember Jesus knew exactly who He was to His Father. Despite knowing His three years would end hung on a cross, beaten and humiliated, He never wavered from what He was sent to earth to do. I'm blown away daily by the magnitude of knowing this! Jesus and His disciples are on their way from

Jerusalem to Galilee. Going through Samaria is a direct route, but oftentimes people would travel out of their way to avoid going through Samaria.

To give you some quick historical context for our time today, I'm going to give you some quick facts about the Samaritans. When the Babylonians captured Judah, they took almost all the Israelite population captive, exiling them to the Babylonian empire. Behind they left those they felt were the lowest class or those deemed too poor to live in Babylonia. Those left behind would intermarry with foreigners moving into the region. Samaritans emerged as a new ethnic group. While they had a historical connection to the people of Israel, their faith was a combination of commands and rituals from the law of Moses, mixed with other foreign religions. There was a lot of tension in that time between the Jews and the Samaritans. They were seen as Biblically uneducated in the eyes of the Israelites, specifically the Pharisees. Who teaches people the Bible? The Pharisees and Rabbis.

What do you think it was like to be a Samaritan in Jesus' day?

What did we learn about the past of the woman at the well through her interaction with Jesus? (vs 17).

What identities do you think she carries?

I love how John writes in verse 4 that Jesus had to go through Samaria. We know He didn't have to, it wasn't the only route to Galilee. But Jesus will always go out of His way, no matter what time of day it is to give someone the opportunity to encounter Him. Jesus arrives at the well around the sixth hour, which is around noon, the hottest time of the day. He is tired and thirsty so He sits to rest. I love that even though we know Jesus is the living water and the bread of life, we see glimpses of His humanness throughout His ministry. He often uses it to lead people to something better, something eternal.

The Samaritan woman approaches the well as Jesus sits there resting and He asks her for a drink of water. The woman is at the well in the hottest part of the day for a reason. Most went to the well in the late afternoon as the weather cooled off. Not only to collect water, but it was a time when the community would gather. Given what we know about the woman, it's easy to assume that she's come to the well, alone, at a time when she hopes to collect water and not run into anyone. How often do we avoid places of community when we're hiding shame in our lives? People in her village know the lifestyle she's led. There's nothing she can do to change that, but she can avoid being at the well when much of the village is there to steer clear of overhearing gossip. Quite possibly she's avoiding dirty looks from the other men and women.

It's so much easier to cast the first stone on someone else's sin, while completely ignoring our own, isn't it? That's why, just like Jesus knew what this woman needed, He knows that we do too. Ok, I've hopped on a tangent, let's get back to the story because it's so beautiful and it's the perfect example of how an encounter with Jesus, allowing Him to name us and love on us, then leads to us walking passionately in our calling. Jesus' interaction with the woman at the well shows us that our past mistakes: shame, guilt, and sin, will never disqualify us from being used by God. In fact, it's our freedom and deliverance from these areas that lead others to find Jesus. There's no hiding from Jesus. He wants to expose all we hide in the deepest parts of us. Not to shame us, but to heal us.

In verses 10-15, Jesus tells the women, "if you know the gift of God and who it is that asks you for a drink, you would have asked him and he would have given you living water." Living water is moving water, like a river or a stream. It's not stagnant, it flows with direction and intention. You will never truly encounter Jesus and leave stagnant. That's what He's communicating to this woman. The water in her well is stagnant, much like her life, but He has come to bring new life! Then we see something so beautiful happen. This woman is beginning to understand that she's not encountering just any Jewish man at the well, but maybe this is Christ the Savior they had heard about.

Jesus answered her, "If you knew the gift of God and who it is that asks you for a drink, you would have asked him and he would have given you living water."

John 4:10

Write John 4:15 (NIV)

The woman said to him, "Sir, _____ _____ this water so that I _____ get _____ and have to keep _____ _____ to draw water."

The woman is so desperate to not ever have to come back to this place where she has experienced so much humiliation and pain. She asks for water that will never bring her back to the well. Jesus didn't want to take the well away from her, He wanted to strip from her what the well had become for her. He doesn't beat around the bush. He knows she needs this moment to break free from what she had been carrying. Jesus asks her to go get her husband. Yet, she doesn't have one and He knows it. She's had multiple husbands and is currently living with one who she's not married to. The final transformational moment for her is this one when Jesus calls her out and "reads her mail" about her past. How could He possibly know all these things?

Our strength for our calling comes from meeting Jesus at the well and allowing Him to break us free from things that have bound us. It's from this place of healing we can fully lean into how He wants to use us to multiply the kingdom. The greatest commission is to go out and make disciples of all nations (Matthew 28). That's exactly what He's doing here. Going through Samaria, not around, to meet this woman where she's at. To risk being seen alone with a Samaritan woman. At the well at the hottest part of the day, so she can have an encounter with Him because He had a bigger plan for her life. Plans to prosper her and use her to multiply His kingdom.

I love that Jesus not only leads us to living water, but He does it by being the greatest example. Yesterday we talked about Jesus in the wilderness being tempted by Satan after fasting for 40 days and 40 nights. While Jesus is God, He still had also spent 30 years on earth, by this point, as a man. He encountered the same temptations we do. What we see in those 40 days is His Father preparing Him for His next three years of ministry. God stripped Jesus of any humanness, so He would be able to stand guard against the enemy. When we can do that when we feel the weakest, imagine what we're capable of in full strength. Likewise, He's stripping this woman of her shame and she becomes the first female evangelist in the New Testament.

WEEK 3 | PASSION

Write John 4:26.

Diving Deeper

How do you resonate with the woman at the well? What impacts you most about Jesus' interaction with her? Do you struggle to believe He would travel "through Samaria" to get to you?

_____

_____

_____

_____

_____

_____

When we encounter Jesus, He gives us our passion, but it must first begin by being passionate about being in relationship with Him. God created you on purpose, for a purpose, but He wants you to lean on Him and drink from His living water. What He has to offer is so much more than you could ever hope for or imagine. The stories in the Bible we read aren't made up so we can read them and feel good about ourselves. His word is living and breathing, those stories are there so we can know that we have full access to those same promises! Amen!!

Posture of Prayer

Today in our journal time, let's spend some time in gratitude, thanking Jesus for meeting us exactly where we are at. Begin to thank Him for His goodness and His faithfulness, and for areas of your life where He has brought freedom. Thank Him for the doors He's opened and the ones He has promised He will open. Thank Him for the example of the woman at the well, so we can know we have the same access to the living water He offers.

(BE)KNOWN

DAY FOUR

In the fall of 2021, I joined a women's Bible study going through the book of Judges. The woman leading it is incredibly anointed. Honestly, I would've studied any book of the Bible we were going through, but I walked in on night one having no idea what to expect from studying Judges. I was in a season of holding tightly to the promises God had spoken over me. Yet I was beginning to question if I was the right "fit" for the calling. I had begun pitching my book to agents, which brought a whole new level of vulnerability and I felt like the enemy was attacking from all sides. He was having a lot of success keeping me from completing many aspects of my book proposal. I know it may seem so small, but how do you translate your purpose, passion, and personality into 500 words and a photo and call it a bio? To me, it just seemed like a mountain I was struggling to climb, but it was needed to submit my proposal to the agents I was meeting with.

I think it was the second month of studying Judges and Beth was preaching about Gideon. God had so clearly called him and told him he would have the victory, yet Gideon still questioned God. Three times he asked for confirmation that God would lead his army to defeat their enemy. Three times, the Lord met Gideon where he was and gave him the confirmation he needed. Beth looked up from her notes, took off her glasses, and in that moment, I felt like she was looking directly at me when she said, "if you know God has called you, but

WEEK 3 | PASSION

you are wavering on walking confidently in it, I dare you to ask Him for three confirmations." I didn't hesitate, I told the Lord right then and there, "if you're calling me to lead women into your presence and teach them how to fall in love with your Word, give me three confirmations.... In the next 24 hours." Bold, I know. But, do you know what? He gave them to me. The first one came from a woman I didn't know that very same night. The second was from a woman I've known for a long time and the third was from Beth the next day! I haven't looked back since.

YOU ARE UNIQUELY GIFTED

We're going to wrap up the story of the woman at the well today, but there are a couple key points I want you to take away from our time together.

1. God has given each of us a unique fingerprint and a unique calling to multiply His kingdom. No one is more gifted, they're uniquely gifted. God has a plan for each one of our lives.

2. Every purpose God gives us is to be used for the benefit of others.

3. You can't live in your calling without a hunger and thirst for the Holy Spirit.

Which one did you need to be reminded of today?

Are you ready to get started? I don't know about you, but talking about how each one of us was designed by our Creator for a unique purpose makes me all kinds of excited.

Let's read John 4: 28-42 together.

What does the woman leave behind? (vs 28) _____

When we find freedom in Jesus, we will leave what once burdened us, at the feet of Jesus. As the disciples rejoin Jesus, He has just finished His conversation with the women at the well. No longer weighed down from all the identities she had once carried, she leaves Jesus with a renewed passion. In one conversation, she found freedom. She found her identity. She fell in love with Jesus and she became passionate about telling others what she had experienced. Jesus had to go through Samaria because He knew how many people would come to know Him and believe in Him because of this woman.

This takes us straight back to our first point: God has given each of us a unique fingerprint and a unique calling to multiply His kingdom. God has a plan for each of our lives. Jesus knew what she needed that day. He knew all she was carrying when she went to the well, but He also knew what she was capable of if she had an encounter with Him. I want us to look up a few scriptures together that I know will encourage us as we chase after the calling Jesus has put on our hearts.

Isaiah 64:8 (NIV)

"Yet you, LORD, are our Father. We are the _____, you are the _____; we are all the _____ of your hand."

Jeremiah 1:4-5 (NIV)

"The _____ of the Lord came to me, saying, "Before I _____ you in the womb I _____ you, before you were born I set you apart; I _____ you as a prophet to the nations."

Ephesians 2:10 (NIV)

"For we are _____ _____, created in Christ Jesus for good works, which God _____ beforehand, that we should _____ in them."

Psalm 139:16 (NIV):

"Your eyes _____ my _____ body; all the days _____ for me were _____ in your book _____ one of them came to be."

WEEK 3 | PASSION

I love these verses so much. They're the most precious reminder that Jesus created you, and He knows you. He has given your life meaning, has a plan for your life and He wants to help you walk in it. If you have an extra minute, go back and re-read those verses again, this time speaking them out loud over yourself. There is so much power in doing this because God's Word is alive!

After the woman leaves her water jug behind at the well, she immediately goes back to the place that has caused her so much agony. The source of the baggage she carried was her village. This time as she enters the town, something is different. She proclaims, "Come, see a man who told me everything I ever did." No longer bound by shame, she has found freedom and a calling. She becomes one of the first women to evangelize about Jesus.

What do the people in the town do after she tells them about Jesus? (vs 39)

Yes, they come out of the town and make their way to the well to see Jesus. This takes us back to the very heart of my second point for today — every purpose God gives us is to be used for the benefit of others. How beautiful and redemptive this moment must've been for this woman. The woman who once was the source of town gossip, who tried to stay hidden and avoid people in her town, is now standing in the middle of it. Inviting everyone to come and have the same experience with Jesus she did! It doesn't matter to Jesus if you work in the marketplace, work from home, a mother home with your children, single, married, divorced, widowed, our Creator has a plan for your life. One to use you to multiply His kingdom. Whatever He calls you to do, it will always be to benefit others around you.

Read Habakkuk 2:3-4 in the margin, what dreams is He putting on your heart as we've talked about finding our purpose this week? Let's write them down!

If you felt it was difficult to answer the questions above, take some time to meditate on Habakkuk 2:3-4 and ask the Lord to reveal them to you. In my valley moments I experienced throughout the last couple of years, I clung to the

> *For the revelation awaits an appointed time; it speaks of the end and will not prove false. Though it linger, wait for it; it will certainly come and will not delay. "See, the enemy is puffed up; his desires are not upright but the righteous person will live by his faithfulness.*
>
> *Habakkuk 2:3-4*

promise of this scripture. I kept seeking after the Lord for patience as I waited on His perfect timing.

I want to touch on one more point before we close today because it's so vital to our walk with Jesus. We can't live in our calling without a hunger and thirst for the Holy Spirit to be actively moving in our lives. There's nothing more beautiful than the aroma of Jesus. We are who we spend time with, don't you want people to smell the Lord's sweet fragrance all over you? I know I do!! Pour it out Jesus over your daughters, from the top of their heads to the soles of their feet.

Let's look back at verse 34. The disciples are encouraging Jesus to eat so He does not go hungry as He speaks to the people of the town. Just like Jesus tells the woman at the well that if she truly knew Him, she would not need to come to the well for stagnant water, she would ask for living water. Jesus begins speaking about food. He says, "My food is to do the will of Him who sent me and finish His work." Again, He's taking this moment to take the focus away from temporary, earthly things and set their eyes above. The true source of their strength. Like the living water, He's talking about an eternal crop. Food that can sustain them longer than bread.

When we let the Lord lead our calling, the flame of that passion stays lit longer. We will run the race with endurance because we are focused on quenching our thirst and satisfying our hunger with the power of the Holy Spirit in our lives. Maybe, you're fully walking in your calling or maybe, you're in a season of waiting and writing down the ideas the Lord is giving you. No matter the season, keep your eyes on Jesus to sustain you.

Which of the three points we talked about today was a confirmation from the Holy Spirit for the season of walking in your purpose you're currently in? Why?

John 4:39 says, "Many of the Samaritans from that town believed in him because of the woman's testimony." How do we know? Not just because they witnessed the power of Jesus that day. They witnessed how the power of Jesus can transform the life of a woman who said, "I once was this, but then I encountered Jesus and now I am this! Come, experience it for yourself." She encountered Jesus, found her identity in who He said she was, and He gave her a purpose and a calling. Because of that calling, she benefited the body of Christ and was a part of multiplying His kingdom from that day forward. They responded to the woman's testimony, "we no longer believe just because of what you have said; now we have heard for ourselves, and we know that this man really is the Savior of the world." Hallelujah!

Diving Deeper

When have you gone through a season of waiting on the Lord for Him to open doors for you to walk in the calling He has put on your heart? What did you do in the waiting? How has that helped sustain you for the season you're in now? If you're still waiting for the Lord to open those doors, how has today encouraged you? How will you approach God as you wait?

_____

_____

_____

_____

Abraham waited 100 years for the son God promised Him. The Israelites wandered in the desert for 40 years to get to the promised land. Noah spent 120 years building an ark in preparation for the flood. Daniel was in the lion's den for 3 days (may not seem like a long time, but if you're in the company of lions, it can seem like eternity. Can I get an amen?) Moses waited his entire life to lead the Israelites into God's promise. Jesus was 30 before His ministry began. Do you hear what I'm saying right now? We will walk in our calling, using the gifts God has given us, we just need to be willing to use them in every season of our lives.

Posture of Prayer

Grab your prayer journal and spend some time talking to Jesus. We covered a lot of ground today, I'm so proud of you and so is He. If you're struggling with one of the 3 areas we talked about today, talk to Jesus about it. Begin praying and declaring His favor and blessing over your calling. Ask for those doors to fling wide open!

DAY FIVE

During the pandemic, let's be real, we were all online a lot. I'm pretty sure my average daily screen time, at one point, was over nine hours a day. Ouch! You know how even after your babies are grown, you still rock the Target shopping cart when you're waiting in the checkout line? Well, let's just say my fingers were in the scrolling position even when I wasn't online. For several months I found myself spending a lot of time on a newly released social media app that was almost like having access to virtual conferences, and enabled you to learn from and connect with people all over the world. It was on that app I ended up meeting other Christian women, talking about faith, sharing miracle stories, and pouring over scripture. God opened the doors for new friendships with other female believers all over the world in a time when we needed to be encouraging one another. It was there that I met Samantha and Avery and Kara.

There was an instant Godly connection! We all got to meet in person when Avery put on a women's faith-based conference. She invited Kara, Samantha, and me to speak. As I got to know Kara and Samantha, God had really been teaching me a lot about living abundantly and what that looks like as a daily

WEEK 3 | PASSION

practice. I had created an Instagram account, "Called to Abundance," (now Be Together Collective) where I was sharing what the Lord was teaching me. God had put the same message of abundance on the hearts of these ladies too. Kara had an account called Abundance Mama (now HAVN app) and Samantha has Abundant Woman Co. It would've been so easy to see them as competition to what I felt God was calling me to share with women online, but instead it knitted us together. It doesn't mean we never had a vulnerable conversation about it. Isn't it the beauty of God that when He calls us to something and our first love is Him, we're able to find camaraderie with other women He's given the same message to, rather than giving in to the feeling we need to compete with them? Even two years later, we're still cheering each other on.

REMAINING IS ESSENTIAL TO THE CALLING

Can you believe this week is almost over? I praise Jesus for all of you and your commitment to study scripture and lean fully into all that God has for you. It is such a gift to be able to join with other women, linking arms and chasing after Jesus together.

In what ways do you feel the Lord has transformed your life this week as we've studied the scriptures together?

Read 1 John 2:27 (NKJV) and write it below.

"But the _____ which _____ have _____ from Him _____ in you, and you do not need that anyone teach you; but as the same _____ _____ you concerning all things, and is true, and is not a lie, and just as it has taught you, you will _____ in Him"

What does the word abide mean to you?

Now take a moment to look up the definition of Abide, what does it mean?

The definition of abide is, "to remain stable or fixed in a state." It is used almost 80 times in the Bible, many of which occur in the gospel of John (34 times) and in his letters (19) times. It doesn't just appear in the New Testament, but in the Old Testament as well. One of the first references to abiding in God is in 1 Samuel 1 when Hannah goes to the temple. She is pleading desperately with God to carry a baby of her own. She tells the Lord, that if He gave her a son, she would dedicate him back to the Lord and he would abide with the Lord in His temple.

Remaining is so essential to our calling. It's what tethers us to our Creator so we can hear His voice and listen for the strategies He's going to give us so we can walk confidently in our purpose. When we get distracted looking to the left and to the right, we allow comparison to creep in. Comparison leads to jealousy and envy, which eventually leads to the inward feeling that we need to compete with the women around us for our spot at the table. The good news is, sweet friends, God has already set the table and there's already a place setting at the table with your name etched in gold.

Write John 15:4 below.

Ladies, if you want to bear Godly fruit, the kind of fruit that leads you into His glory, and will bring kingdom impact and multiplication, you have to remain in Jesus. That looks like prioritizing spending time in His presence: praying, fasting, reading the Word, and memorizing scripture. When we

WEEK 3 | PASSION

know Jesus, we become less concerned with whose doors are opening before ours because the only doors we want to walk through are the ones that God is opening for us! I was reading Mark Batterson's 40 days of Prayer one summer with some friends as we were praying specifically for our businesses. The week that I was praying that the Lord would begin bringing introductions to book agents, Mark was talking about the power of Jesus as a networker.

Have you ever heard the phrase, we're six degrees of separation from someone we want to meet? If we're six degrees, then our Creator is one degree away from everyone because He created us all! I loved reading that so much and it convicted my heart with its truth. It's almost like saying, if you're looking to "level up," get on your knees every morning and remain in God's presence because He's connected to more people than anyone else you'll ever meet. He can bring divine appointments you might've missed if you were busy running ahead of Him.

Abiding in Jesus requires us to put blinders on. Have you ever been to a horse race or watched one on tv? All the horses have blinders on the outside of their eyes, forcing them to only look forward to what's directly in front of them. Jockeys do this so that the horses don't get spooked, distracted, or concerned with what the other horses in the race are doing. They can solely focus on the commands of the Jockey. We need to put our spiritual blinders on so that we can stay focused on the race that God has set before us and do it with excellence, never lacking in zeal.

My heart is for this day to encourage you and to remind you that your calling, just like your fingerprints are uniquely for you, and only you. The longer you lean into the distractions of the world, the more you will find yourself frustrated and the enemy will begin to find his way into those spaces of your heart and make you feel as though you can't be used by God. Take captive that lie, friend, there's nothing further from the truth. Here is some truth to stand on as you wait in the Lord's presence for Him to give you the blueprints for what He's calling you to. You can't be frustrated if you feel like God isn't speaking to you or opening those doors if you're not prioritizing time with Him every single day. If He doesn't have your first fruits, how can you expect your fruit to bloom on the vine?

If He doesn't have your first fruits, how can you expect your fruit to bloom on the vine?

HOW WE DO IT	SCRIPTURE
Know your Creator	Genesis 1:26-28
Discipline your body	1 Corinthians 9:27
Guard your heart	Proverbs 4:23
Don't gossip	Proverbs 20:19
Mind your own business	1 Thessalonians 4:11
Renew your mind	Romans 12:2
Do your own good works	Ephesians 2:10
Focus on your own salvation	Philippians 2:12

HOW WE DO IT	SCRIPTURE
Run our own race	1 Corinthians 9:24-27
Dig your own well	Genesis 26:23-25
Tend your own field	Proverbs 20:4
Confess your own sin	James 5:16
Build your own house	Matthew 7:24-27
Protect your own eyes	Matthew 6:22
Manage your own household	1 Timothy 3:4-5
Pay close attention to your own doctrine	1 Timothy 4:16

As you look over this list, which area(s) do you find distract you from walking confidently in your purpose?

I want to encourage you to grab some post-it notes or 3x5 cards and write down the verses for those areas you listed above and begin to read them out loud, pray and declare them over your life. We were not created for competition, we were created for collaboration. The world celebrates pitting women against each other, but God's calling us to live an opposite life from those of this world. When you abide in Him and find your confidence in what He has called you to and His timing to do it, you will look for ways to honor the other women in your life and cheer them on as they walk in the calling God has for them. This is why I love listening to other women preach the Word of God.

How are you going to abide in Jesus daily, starting today?

If you're looking for a way to create a beautiful space to dive into the Bible each morning and dig your well, my friend Jane Johnson has a beautiful study called, The School of Scripture. It has even helped me transform my time in the Word each morning. I highly recommend you grab a copy for yourself!

Diving Deeper

What does your time with Jesus look like? Is it a priority? How are you giving Him the first fruits of your day so He can prosper the rest? How is Jesus convicting you to make some adjustments to how you spend time with him daily?

_____

_____

_____

_____

_____

I cannot wait to hear from you about how your new routine of abiding in Jesus daily has changed your relationship with Jesus and given you a renewed passion for your calling. I declare Isaiah 43:18-19 over you, "Forget the former things, do not dwell (abide) on the past. See, I am doing a new thing! Now it springs up; do you not perceive it? I am making a way in the desert and streams in the wasteland." When we enter God's presence, we never leave the same. And it's so beautiful! What God has for us, no man (or woman) alone can give us.

Posture of Prayer

Spend some time journaling and praying for those areas where you don't have your spiritual blinders on. Begin declaring those scriptures in prayer, asking the Lord to meet you in those places and begin to transform you from the inside out, that His beautiful aroma would follow you wherever you go because you've chosen to abide in Him, in all things! Amen!

uniquely gifted

WEEK FOUR

Can you believe we're already halfway through our time together?

I'm so proud of you! Even I had moments while writing this study where the Lord revealed new areas that I had focused on myself and not Him and was convicted to leave those things at His feet. I want you to know you are uniquely gifted and wired by God for specific service in His kingdom and His Church! We are taking a deep dive into Spiritual gifts this week, and I hope you complete the Spiritual gifts test in our homework this week. Sometimes you may doubt it, but the Word of God promises that you have been given gifts. Some of these gifts will be used in your home or marketplace and some will benefit working and serving alongside others in the Church. We are going to talk this week about people like Ezra and Esther who stepped out in faith when they had begun to discover what they had been uniquely designed for by God.

The call to flourish in our gifting for Jesus and His mission, can come with challenges. We may find ourselves struggling with feeling God's not using us in the way and time we hoped. We will look at areas we need to re-learn to trust God's timing for our lives so we can cheer on other women in their callings, even in our seasons of waiting. It could be that past church hurts have held you back from being part of a church community again, but I want to encourage you to find a church to be planted in! The church needs you and your gifts. It's God's greatest desire that we can walk boldly and confidently in who He says you are and the calling on your life so He can use the gifts He's uniquely gifted you with to expand the kingdom of Heaven. Let's get into this together, because God has so much to say about the beautiful way He has designed you and the exciting plans He has in mind for you. Let's learn what it means to say "Yes" to Him!

LIVE BOLDLY IN HIM,

group discussion

Take some time to worship together. We have included a worship playlist in the appendix if you need guidance on a song to pick this week.

introduction

You are unique. There are things that you can do that other people can't do. And, here's the crazy thing about that – you might not even know what you're good at because it comes so naturally to you. In this week's session, we're going to help you discover how God has uniquely gifted you to serve others.

come together

Open your group with prayer. This should be a brief, simple prayer in which you invite God to be with you as you meet.

As we have said in previous lessons, sharing our personal stories builds deeper connections among group members. Your story may be exactly what another person needs to hear, and listening to others' stories is an act of love and kindness to them—and could very well help them to grow spiritually. Begin your time together by using the following questions and activities to get people talking.

- What have others told you about your natural gifts and talents?

- Who do you know that truly demonstrates a servant's heart? Why do you think so?

WEEK 4 | UNIQUELY GIFTED

watch video session 4
beknownbiblestudy.com/videos

group discussion

grow together

Read Romans 11:29 (AMP)

For the gifts and the calling of God are irrevocable [for He does not withdraw what He has given, nor does He change His mind about those whom He sends His call.

Have someone Read 1 Corinthians 12:7-11

- What spiritual gifts are you aware of having? How has God used you to bless others with these gifts?

- When you think of your roles in your family, at work, or at church, what do you love to do?

- What needs in your community concern you the most? What could you do about it?

be together

Let's dive deeper into what it means to be uniquely gifted. God interwove gifts when He created you, but we often get sidetracked wanting to thrive in the giftings we see others use, we lose sight of the ones the Lord has given us. How do we rediscover what it looks like to lean fully into our own unique gifts and be willing to use them to build the kingdom of heaven?

- If you knew you couldn't fail, what would you attempt to do for God?

- What excites you about using the gifts God has given you?

- What's maybe a little intimidating about using your gifts?

Groups grow closer when they serve together. How could your group serve someone in need? You may want to visit those who are homebound from your church, provide a meal for a family who is going through difficulty, or give some other practical help to someone in need. If nothing comes to mind, spend time praying and asking God to show you who needs your help. Have two or three group members organize a serving project for the group, and then do it!

Close your meeting with prayer.

WEEK 4

daily study

DAY ONE

I remember when my kids were younger, beginning to see glimpses of gifts and talents starting to stand out in each of them. We had gone through a stage where they were signed up for so many different sports and activities: painting classes, soccer, baseball, softball, swimming. Honestly, it wore me out driving them around. Probably as much as it did them. One by one, the kids would lose interest and not want to be part of that sport or activity anymore. I had no idea what to do with their disinterest. After all, wasn't it my job as a mother to help them discover their gifts and talents and help them pursue them? I would sit in conversations with other moms whose kids seemed to be excelling at every sport, in every season, and it seemed as though neither one of my children had latched onto anything. In those moments it became so easy to compare them with other kids their age. The Lord reminded me in my quiet times with Him that it wasn't my job to bring those gifts out of them, it was His.

The best thing I could ever do was to pray for each of them that they would begin to see the gifts God has given them and how He was going to use them. As soon as I began to surrender them to what the Lord had for them and I stopped trying to sign them up for everything, our son quit baseball (truly I loved it more than he did). He picked up soccer and the joy he exudes when he plays, along with the skill that God has given him, has opened the doors for some wonderful opportunities for him. Coaches love to coach him because he's teachable, a team player and he will play any position and give it 100%. Our daughter tried out for a musical to get more involved in school and landed a lead part! We hadn't

WEEK 4 | UNIQUELY GIFTED

even realized how much she enjoyed singing and acting. She's had several leadership roles since. I don't say this to spark comparison between you and me as we study God's Word together. What I'm hoping you will receive from this story is the beauty of surrendering our kids to their Creator because He is the one who knows all their unique gifts and talents and how He plans to use them.

YOU ARE UNIQUELY GIFTED

In the last few weeks, we've talked about the invitation to be in an intimate relationship with Jesus, who He says we are and His calling for our lives. With that calling comes the giftings, both natural and supernatural He has given us to walk our calling here on earth. There is no shortage of ways your Creator plans to use you if you're ready to stay surrendered to His plan and His timing. I don't know about you, but the timing part is always the hard one for me. Whether you're naturally a go-getter, type a personality, or more laid back and patient, I think we can all agree that when it comes to the Lord's timing, sometimes an extra dose of patience is needed. Can I take a moment to encourage you? It's worth the wait! His plans to use your gifts are always so much more than you can ever anticipate or imagine. Friend, choose to walk with Him, not in front of Him along the way.

If you had to list out some of your strengths, what would you say? List them in the margin.

my Strengths are...

Let's read Romans 12:4-8 together.

Which of the gifts Paul lists in these scriptures align with the strengths you listed in the margin?

Which one(s) do you feel you use daily?

Which one(s) do you wish you used more?

Let's read 1 Corinthians 12:7-11 together.

How do you feel about the supernatural gifts Paul talks about? Do you believe God still uses them within us today?

Which of these gifts do you feel the Lord has used/is using in your life?

Write 1 Corinthians 12:4 in the space below.

Remember when we talked about Deborah's gift of prophecy, which is, another word for encouraging or edifying those around you? In the supernatural, the use of that same gift of prophecy is to give someone the wisdom they need to affirm them in what God's calling them to. There is a divine connection between how the Lord uses our gifts in the natural and the supernatural. Did you see that connection when you shared your strengths and the gifts Paul lists in Romans and 1 Corinthians?

That's why He gave us the power of the Holy Spirit! The Biblical definition of 'supernatural', according to Strong's Dictionary, means "beyond, or exceeding, the power of laws of nature; miraculous." It's through the power of the Holy Spirit, given to us when we accept Jesus into our lives and turn away from our old lives, that allows us to use the gifts. They're all built into our DNA, but some of them we exercise naturally and others we need to ask the Lord to begin bringing them out in us.

Our natural gifts are the ones we're born with — like my son's athletic ability or my daughter's singing and acting abilities. Our supernatural ones come when we encounter Jesus as our Savior and truly surrender our lives to His plan. We're not believers because we grew up in a Christian home, went to a Christian school, or attend church on Sunday. None of those will give you the key to Heaven. It's when you give your heart fully to Jesus that your relationship with Him becomes yours. It's personal, it's beautiful and the result is falling in love with Him and

WEEK 4 | UNIQUELY GIFTED

craving time in His presence. When you love someone--a parent, grandparent, boyfriend, husband,--you want to spend every waking moment you have with them. It should feel the same when you spend time with Jesus.

Jesus has never stopped desiring to spend time with you. Amen! Aren't you so thankful we have a Creator that never stops chasing after our hearts? Who never wants to stop being included in our dreams. Who wants to give us all the desires of our heart, as long as those desires are kingdom focused. And ladies, getting married and having children falls into that, so long as you're not settling for less than what God has intended for you.

When was the last time you felt that way about Jesus?

In week one we talked about the invitation Jesus gives us to step into deeper intimacy with Him. **Take a moment to write a letter or journal an invitation to Jesus letting Him know how much you love Him and how you want to be more intentional about spending time with Him. What do you want it to look like in your life?**

_____

_____

_____

_____

Let's read Matthew 6:33 (NIV) together:

"But _____ first the _____ of _____ and _____ _____, and all these things shall be _____ to you."

When we are kingdom focused — chasing after an intimate relationship with Jesus, putting Him first in all things, we will begin to see the fruit of that in our lives. It will come out through the fruit of the Spirit (Galatians 5:22), but also in how God uses our gifts.

I want to take a few minutes to have us all take a spiritual gifts test. There are many different types of gifts tests you can take, but I love this one because your spiritual gifts are an extension of your natural ones. For example, if you have the gift of teaching or coaching — your spiritual gift might be knowledge. Maybe you love to bring people together and you love to host and have gatherings in your home — your gift might be hospitality. Grab your computer, iPad, tablet, or your preferred device and pop over to the website below. The test should only take about 5-7 minutes. It's all digital and you'll get your results right away.

www.biblesprout.com/articles/god/holy-spirit/spiritual-gifts-test

What were your top three gifts? _____

Which one surprised you the most? _____

What gift/gifts are you already using? _____

Which one do you want to ask the Lord to begin using in and through you in a greater way? _____

How do you see God using these gifts in your life, not just serving in the church?
_____

I pray that through taking this test that the Lord begins to affirm and confirm in mighty ways, not only our giftings but how He wants to use them in and through you. When we use them in tandem, our natural and supernatural gifts are a mighty force against the plans of the enemy. Remember, the enemy comes to steal, kill and destroy, but the Lord gives us LIFE, and life abundantly! That abundant life is not just for our benefit, but for the benefit of those around us. They might be gifts the Lord has given us, but they're given so we can share them with others, that they might too be encouraged and lean into their giftings.

Our natural and supernatural gifts, when we use them in tandem, are a might force against the plans of the enemy.

Read Romans 8:9 (TPT) out loud over yourself.

"But when the Spirit of Christ empowers your life, you are not dominated by the flesh but by the Spirit. And if you are not joined to the Spirit of the Anointed One, you are not of Him." Romans 8:9 (TPT)

Let's live a life that is joined to the Anointed One, that we would be empowered by the Spirit of Christ to use our gifts to benefit the body of Christ.

Diving Deeper

What thoughts do you need to surrender so you can be empowered by the Holy Spirit to use the gifts, both natural and supernatural He has given you? What is a gift that you felt stirring within you as you completed today's reading?

_____

_____

_____

_____

_____

_____

Oftentimes it's our lack of trust that God knows exactly how He plans to use our gifts that holds us back from using them. How do we break free from that? There's only one answer... chase after Him! Give Him the first fruits of your day, the best of your day. Create space for quiet moments with Him, maybe that's 60-90 minutes before everyone in your house wakes up, maybe it's in the middle of the day when the kids are napping, or right before you go to bed. Relationships flourish in intentional intimacy building. Be intentional in how you chase after Jesus and I promise you will begin to see Him use the gifts you have and ones you never realized you had.

Posture of Prayer

Take some time to ask the Lord to begin activating your gifts in you. Maybe you're already walking in some of them, thank Him and ask Him to keep showing you and opening doors for you to use those gifts to glorify the Kingdom. Maybe you feel like you're still waiting on the Lord, thank Him for the extra time with Him to be prepared for how He plans to use your gifts.

(BE) KNOWN

DAY TWO

A couple of years ago my husband and I were invited to a President's weekend for an organization called the Illuminations Foundation. Ten different non-profits focused on Bible translation came together to see how they could leverage the technology they had built, relationships they had established, and work they each had already done to get the gospel of Jesus translated into every heart language. Before they came together the predicted date of completion was 2050 or later, but now it's closer to 2030. Hallelujah! I cannot even begin to imagine what it would be like to not have the living, breathing Word of God at my fingertips. The weekend was incredible! An outpouring of passion for worship and the Word of God, but there was no mistaking the thankfulness and generosity we felt throughout our time there. With the backdrop of Ojai Valley, hundreds of us gathered to listen to people who are risking their lives all over the world to help translate the Word of God into their heart language because they don't want anyone to miss out on Heaven.

It brought new meaning to what it looks like to live a bold life of faith! At the end of the weekend, they shared a map of the world that showed where there are *pockets of people who do not know about Jesus and that moment changed my heart. It transformed me in a way I wasn't expecting. Yes, I knew in the back of my mind that there were people who didn't have access to the Bible but seeing that map gave me a visual of truth, glaring back at me, with a beautiful invitation to be part of changing that. The Lord gave me a number He wanted us to give as a financial gift almost immediately and it was beyond what I had initially been thinking. So much so that I didn't even want to share it with Kyle. That afternoon as we took a walk, soaking up the sunshine, we looked at each other and shared the same number God had given each of us. It wasn't just a gift. For us, it was a sacrificial gift. Yet we gave it, joyfully! The following week the Lord brought us a new client and 10% of the budget was what we had given! It's so beautiful what happens when we hold our earthly treasure loosely because we know it belongs to Jesus. And friend, I can tell you so many more stories like that one!*

WELLS IN THE DESERT

Yesterday we talked about our gifts, both natural and supernatural. My prayer, sweet friend, is that taking the Spiritual gifts test stirred something new and unexpected inside you. One of my favorite Bible verses and one I've clung to, spoken aloud, and prayed over myself is Isaiah 43:18-19. I've written it in the margin for you. It's a bold declaration of a beautiful promise over us, "I (God) am doing a new thing in you [add your name here], do you not perceive it? I am making a way in the desert." So often our journey of patience as we wait on the Lord to take our passion and our purpose and turn it into our calling can feel like a desert. But where there is a desert, there is always a well! Where God leads, He will also sustain us in the waiting.

After all, no one modeled being in the presence of the Heavenly Father, more than Jesus himself. He knew His identity, His purpose, and His calling. He always lived in the light of eternity. Jesus knew that He came, not so He could be lifted up as royalty, crowned with jewels and rule over nations, but that we might have life! This goes back to the living water we talked about in week two. Where His presence is, so is the bread of life and living water to sustain us, nurture us, and love us with an agape (a deep, unconditional love) love, that is so deep and so wide, that we might not ever understand the full extent of it till we are with Jesus in Heaven.

Forget the former things; do not dwell on the past. See, I am doing a new thing! Now it springs up; do you not perceive it? I am making a way in the wilderness and streams in the wasteland.

Isaiah 43:18-19

Share anything that the Lord has stirred up in you since yesterday as you think about your gifts. Be sure to put a date on this day so you can come back and visit what God has done since you wrote it.

Lord, I pray that you would seal the words my sweet friend has shared above and you would begin to increase that stirring in her heart to lean into what you have next for her. I pray you would begin to bring new ideas, new blueprints, and open doors for kingdom collaborations that affirm the calling on her life. That this Bible study would serve as a launching pad for all that you have for her. Let her dream dreams and see visions of how you will use her in her home, in her community, amongst her friends, at her church and in the marketplace to bring these dreams and visions to pass. We thank you for your agape love, Jesus. - Amen

Today we're going to look at the three ways we use our gifts to build the kingdom of Heaven. Kingdom collaboration boils down to three things: your time, talent, and treasure. As I was praying over today, I felt the Lord saying so strongly that He wants to shift our thinking and show us what being kingdom-minded looks like. We can show Jesus in a secular workplace without saying His name, but emulating Him in action. Similarly, we don't need to wait till our children are a certain age before we can model true discipleship to them. Being kingdom minded is simple. If you know Jesus intimately because you've spent time in His Word and His presence, then the fruit that comes from Him will pass through you like a sweet aroma to everyone around you. It's really easy to speak the Word of God, but if we don't live it out daily, how are we benefiting the kingdom?

I have a love/hate relationship with social media. On one hand, it has brought some of the most beautiful people from all over the world into my life. On the other hand, it has distracted my time, stolen my talent, and buried my treasure. I've had to learn over the years that unless it's bringing peace, joy, and love to those who scroll across my feed (and to me), sometimes it's better to be silent or share someone else's words of wisdom.

WEEK 4 | UNIQUELY GIFTED

Do you have distractions in your life that keep you from living out your calling using your gifts? Maybe, you're like me and it's social media, or possibly tv shows, friendships, you name it. Remember the enemy is like a thief, he comes to steal, kill and destroy and he would love nothing more than to feed you distractions that eat up your time. He wants to make you question the gift God created in you from the time He formed you and encourage you to sink your treasure into things of this world.

If you're taking an honest look at your life, what are some of the things in your life you know are distractions?

God wants us to stay the course. Focus on how we spend our time, and how we use our talent to store up our treasure in Heaven. The Word of God is living and breathing and the Holy Spirit is ready and waiting to activate you in ways you could never dream of. With that in mind, how should we approach our time, talent, and treasure? The Bible is clear about each one of these.

1. Time (personal sacrifice) - 1 John 2:17 (NIV)

"The _____ and its _____ pass away, but whoever does the _____ of God lives forever."

We don't know how long we will have on this earth. The Word says we will not know the time or the date of Jesus' return. What we will stand in account for when we get to Heaven is what we did with our time here on earth. The book of Revelation talks about there being two different books Jesus will open when we get to Heaven (Rev. 20). One is the book of life, in which your name was beautifully written into the day you accepted Jesus into your life. The second book has the story of your life, how you lived, and what you did for the glory of the kingdom. Let's be challenged to spend our lives using our gifts to bring others to Jesus.

What is one thing you're going to give up this next week that takes up much of your time that brings no kingdom fruit? (No saying husbands or kids *wink)

2. Talent (gifts) - James 1:17-18 (TPT)

"Every _____ (or legacy) God _____ _____ us is good and perfect, streaming down from the Father of lights, who shines from the heavens with no hidden shadow or darkness and is never subject to change. God was _____ to _____ us birth by the truth of his infallible Word so that we would _____ his _____ _____ for us and become the _____ ones out of all his creation!"

God's Word doesn't say some gifts from Him are freely given to us and are good and perfect, all of them are. It was His greatest delight as He created us to give us gifts that He will use to fulfill His plan for our lives. I love how The Passion Translation says, "fulfill his destiny for us." Destiny is a predetermined course of events! Just as God created you in His image, He also knows exactly how He wants to use your gifts in the world to help people encounter Him and transform their lives.

What is one gift that you want God to use in your life more?

3. Treasure (financial) - Matthew 6:19-21 (NKJV)

"Do not lay up for yourselves _____ on earth, where moth and rust destroy and where thieves break in and steal; but lay up for yourselves _____ in heaven, where neither moth nor rust destroys and where thieves do not break in and steal. For where your _____ is, there your heart will be also."

This is the point where we all begin to skim the passage, maybe turn the page to find out how close we are to the end of today's homework. Why do we always cringe when it comes to our treasure? Jesus lived a life poured out with generosity. If we desire to truly live like Him, why do we begin to get defensive when we talk about money in the church? There's no getting around the truth, your money is not yours, it's God's. If you're not using it to build the kingdom, then maybe you need to take a moment and take stock of where it's going. If you're spending more money at Starbucks or Target than you are in the kingdom economy, I would like to invite you to sit with Jesus on that one. We want to add jewels to our crowns in heaven, but we're very selective about how we will do it while here on earth. What I love about this passage is that God, in His goodness, is calling us higher. He's reminding us that if our heart is with Him, then generosity with our time, talent, and treasure will be an overflow of our love for Him.

What area(s) of your life do you want to live out generosity this week so you can begin to store up your treasure in heaven?

Diving Deeper

Of the three areas we talked about today, which one is the most difficult one for you to share with others: your time, talent, or treasure? Did the Lord stir up anything in you today to make some changes in that area? How do you want to move forward differently next week?

_____

_____

_____

Oh, friend, I'm so excited we're on this journey together. I can't tell you how many early mornings as I sit here writing, the Lord has convicted my heart as well. He doesn't do it to chastise or shame us, but to invite us into a deeper, more intimate relationship with Him so He can pour out blessings over our lives. Will He bless you even if you choose to continue living the way you are now? Yes, that's what agape (unconditional love) looks like. But imagine how much greater it could be if we learn to love Him with the same intensity He loves us.

Posture of Prayer

Take some time in your journal to thank the Lord for the ways He's going to use your time, talent, and treasure for the Kingdom. Share your struggles or what holds you back with Him and ask Him to help you walk in freedom from those things.

DAY THREE

We lived in Hong Kong around the time I was between the ages of eight and twelve. It was there I discovered my love for ice skating. With only a few lessons I was hooked and I spent those years taking multiple lessons a week and competing. None of my friends from school or church were ice skaters and I loved that it felt like a talent only I had. Every time I went to a competition, yes it was against others, it always just felt as though I was competing against myself. How much better could I perform the routine in competition than I could in practice? At one point, around the age of ten, my coach tried to partner me with a boy for pair skating. Let's just say it didn't go very well and the partnership didn't last very long. I had been skating alone for so long, that I didn't know how to let go of control and allow someone else to lead. The whole process was frustrating for my partner and me. We did manage to eke out one decent and fun Christmas showcase performance. I'm laughing as I write this. Gosh, I was so stubborn!

When I was twelve my Dad came home from work one day and announced we were moving to Kuala Lumpur, Malaysia. I did not take the announcement well! On top of that, there were no ice rinks so my dreams of being an Olympic ice skater were never going to come to fruition. As a twelve-year-old, I was feeling all the feels about changing schools and having to make new friends. Moving this time left me floundering because I didn't know how I was going to find an outlet for what I loved to do. As I met new friends, I found myself *auditioning for the dance team at school. Suddenly, I was competing against friends for a spot on the team and having to push myself to show I was going to be an asset to the team. I thought I would hate it, but it turns out I loved it, and I was good at it. Being surrounded by other girls with the same passion as me, grew me as a person and as a dancer. We might've competed for our spot on the team, but on the team, we brought all of our strengths together and created some of the most memorable dance showcases. I think that's where my love for championing other women began, but it's been because of my growth in the Lord over the years that I've been able to foster it.*

LAYING THE FOUNDATION TOGETHER

Take a moment to read Ezra 3:7-13 with me.

On day three of last week (pg tbd) we talked about the history of Samaria. Do you remember what happened when the Babylonians came in and conquered Judah? They took the Israelites into captivity in Babylon. In the process, the temple had been destroyed. The Israelites remained in captivity for 70 years (608-538 BC) however, some chose to stay longer. In 539 Babylon was captured and King Cyrus, King of Persia came into power.

In the first year of his reign what happens to King Cyrus? (Ezra 1:1)

As a result of being moved by the Spirit of the Lord to fulfill the words spoken by the prophet Jeremiah, King Cyrus proclaims that he is called to rebuild the temple at Jerusalem in Judah. Can you imagine being an Israelite in that moment? Hearing this news. When you think of the lifespan of 70 years, this proclamation went out to those who might've even remembered being taken into captivity along with those who only knew life in captivity. An invitation to come and rebuild the temple of the Lord, where His spirit dwelled in the Ark of the Covenant.

Write Ezra 1:3

King Cyrus goes one step further and he orders the people around the "survivors" (the Israelites in captivity) to give them gold, silver, goods, and livestock as offerings when the temple is complete. As we move on to vs 7 it says that the king also brought out the articles from the temple of the Lord that King Nebuchadnezzar had taken and placed in the temple of his god and gave them back to the Israelites to take with them to Judah. Gosh, I wonder how overwhelming that moment was for them? Perhaps that's why when the invitation to return and build the temple was sent out, many knew immediately they needed to go and others who chose to stay behind in their captivity for another 70 years until the temple was ready to be dedicated.

The truth is, sometimes we would rather stay rooted in what's familiar to us, than step out in faith to use our gifts to build God's house. But friend, what's familiar is not always healthy and those unhealthy habits can bind us and keep us stuck where we're at. Don't let yourself stay bound to those things!

You might be wondering what this has to do with using our gifts. If we're going to talk about using our gifts to build the kingdom and what it means to be a kingdom collaborator, Ezra 3 is a wonderful example. Yet to understand the magnitude of what's happening in the passage we started our day reading, let's look back so we can know what the Israelites had gone through leading up to this moment. It was there the foundation was laid and the celebration began. King Cyrus was so moved by the heart of God that he gave an invitation, not to some, but to all the Israelites to move home and join together using their gifts to rebuild the temple. Much like King Cyrus, Jesus offers us the same invitation.

Remember when we talked about Peter walking on the water? Who was the invitation for in that moment? _____

It was not just for Peter, Jesus said, "come." When He did it was for all of the disciples to step into everything He had for them. Don't focus on the storm, the waves, or the rocking of the boat. Life is always going to be filled with hardship. "Focus on Me," He says. The Israelites had no idea what was awaiting them when they returned. They had no idea where they were going to live, or what they were going to eat, but those who returned knew their God, the same God who would move the heart of the king to give them back their freedom and their land, and would provide for them in their return home as well.

How many people returned to rebuild the temple (Ezra 2:64)? _____

And that number was not even counting the menservants and maidservants and the men and women singers.

When God calls us to use our gifts, He's going to surround us with the people we need to encourage us to live fully in our calling. He's going to open the doors, and provide the materials and the people to work alongside us. But God's also not going to call just you. There are going to be others who He's given similar gifts and called to similar callings. This is where we need to check our pride at the door. Go Google how many people are in the world. Go on, friend, I'll wait here.

7.73 billion (at the time I wrote this)!! It's going to take God giving more than one of us a heart to reach people for His kingdom to reach all those people. We need to link arms with other women to accomplish building the church. Amen!

Write Ezra 3:11 below

It took all the men and women who returned to Jerusalem to work together, side by side to rebuild the temple. Do you think they were concerned about people working next to them who had the same gifts and talents as them? Were they upset that 42,359 other people also returned to help build the temple? No, with joy and gladness they worked together.

How good are you at working side by side with other women who God has given similar callings and gifts? Why do you think that is?

The woman next to you won't steal your calling. Unless you let her. She should inspire you to continue to walk the path the Lord has called you to. She is not you, she will never be you and you will never be her. That's the beauty of it all! It's her unique story that will bring people into the kingdom, but it's also your unique story that will lead others. Imagine how many people we can usher into heaven one day if we all stood together to lay the foundation and then worshiped and praised together.

How do we do this? Write Romans 12:9-12 from The Passion Translation. No matter the translation, this verse is a beautiful representation of how we are to live our lives and use the gifts God has given us.

Romans 12:9-12 (TPT)

"Let the _____ _____ of your heart always be to _____ one another, and _____ play the role of an actor wearing a mask. Despise evil and _____ everything that is good and virtuous. Be _____ to tenderly loving your fellow believers as members of one family. Try to _____ yourselves in respect and _____ of one another. Be _____ to serve the Lord, keeping your _____ toward him boiling hot! _____ with the glow of the Holy Spirit and let him fill you with _____ as you serve him. Let this _____ burst forth within you, releasing a _____ _____. Don't give up in a time of trouble, but commune with God at all times."

The Lord brings me back to the truth of this verse often. God has a plan for your life, He has gifts He's already freely given you from the moment of creation and as we use those gifts we're called to go above and beyond to honor those around us walking that same journey.

Diving Deeper

In what ways is your life an example of kingdom collaboration? Do you struggle with working alongside other women? Where does that stem from?

_____
_____
_____
_____
_____
_____
_____
_____
_____
_____

Whether it's in the church or the marketplace, Jesus wants to use all of us to show the world what it looks like to be in a relationship with Him. Where the world would want to have us work siloed from each other, the Holy Spirit wants to teach us how we can come together. Yes, we are human and some days this is easier said than done and we let the pride of comparison get in the way. It's when we recognize we are reaching that point we need to bring it back to the feet of Jesus and allow Him to reaffirm the gifts He's given us. Then we can fully and beautifully embrace Romans 12:10, to "outdo" each other in honoring others.

Posture of Prayer

Take some time to pray and ask the Lord how He wants to use your gifts to create kingdom collaborations. How does He want you to use your gifts to help others find Him? If there was any part of today that convicted your heart, share that with Him too and ask Him to help you find freedom in those areas.

(BE) KNOWN

DAY FOUR

I've loved teaching for as long as I can remember. Once I knew that was the path I wanted to pursue, I never wavered from it. I graduated with a liberal arts degree, and went on to finish my teaching credential and then my Master's in Education. I taught elementary school and then junior high students until I had our daughter and the Lord called me to be home with her. We had our son a short 17 months later and my life went from teaching in a classroom to teaching myself how to sew and starting a blog. It's crazy to think that was in 2007 before blogging went from black or white backdrops to beautifully designed websites. As I began to connect with people online, my teaching career took a turn. It began with creating a company that partnered bloggers with brands to market their products on their blogs and social media channels. Then teaching bloggers how to successfully pitch themselves to brands and blogging agencies to make an income talking about products and services. It continued when I had opportunities to speak at conferences and teach people how to hire the team you need, how to build a social media presence, and how to work with brands.

In 2019, God began stirring in my heart that He had more in store for me than I could've ever imagined. I had no idea what this meant, but I felt it in the way He began to shift my heart away from a career I had built and back into His Word. For much of the last three years, I felt as though I was walking through a wilderness season.

WEEK 4 | UNIQUELY GIFTED

God would bring me back to the story of Abram and how God called him to go and he went, not knowing where he would settle. He began with obedience and along the way, he built altars and dug wells. So, in obedience, I began worshiping like never before and seeking God for what He had next for me. I didn't see the book coming, let alone this Bible study. If you had told me in 2019 I would write a book called Be Known and a Bible study workbook to compliment it, I would've laughed and told you that you were crazy. I never thought God would open doors for me to teach women about Jesus. We never know how God is going to equip us for our calling, all we can do is walk in obedience, and worship Him on the journey so we can be a living testimony to others along the way. Some days I wish I would've arrived here sooner, but most days I thank Jesus because I know before now, I wouldn't have been ready to serve Him in this way.

YOU ARE LOVELY AND BEAUTIFUL

Today we're going to dive into the story of one of my favorite ladies in the Bible. Yes, I know, I say that about all of them, but it's just so beautiful how the Lord uses women throughout the Bible. In the case of the story of Esther, the gifts God gave her led others to freedom. There's nothing more glorious than being used by God in that way, am I right?

Before we get started today, from memory (no peeking *wink), what do you think Esther's strengths were?

What does the name Esther mean? _____

Esther is the last book part of the historical books in the Bible. While it falls between Nehemiah and Job, if you were to read the Bible in chronological order, Esther falls in the time frame of the end of Zechariah and the last few chapters of Ezra. Not all the Israelites returned to Jerusalem when given the opportunity and now decades later, they're being oppressed under a new king, King Xerxes. Esther was among those who did not return to Jerusalem and was part of the scattered, living through Persia. She was an orphan, both her parents had passed away and she was raised by her cousin Mordecai (Esther 2:7).

Read Esther 1: 1-22

In Esther 1, King Xerxes throws a feast for all the nobles in the surrounding areas. They're eating, drinking, and begin arguing over which of their wives is the most beautiful. Quite possibly intoxicated, which mixes terribly with pride, the king summons his wife, Queen Vashi, to appear before the men to show off her beauty. She refuses to join the party. I wonder if her refusal is less about disrespecting the king, but more about not wanting to be strutted around in a room of drunk men, listening to them debate and make lewd comments. Nevertheless, her refusal to show off for the king's guests results in her being dethroned and banished from ever being in the courts or his presence.

The king is now on the quest to find a new queen and appoints commissioners in every province he rules over to find the most beautiful women in all the land for him to choose from. Esther is selected from among the women to be brought to the citadel for the king. I'm not going to lie, sometimes when I read this book I want to roll my eyes at the king's proclamation to find the most beautiful women in the land, after all, don't they say that beauty is in the eye of the beholder? How would these commissioners even know where to begin?

Then when you peel back the layers, we begin to see where the Lord's favor is all over Esther being elevated to the position of queen. Hadassah, Esther's given name means "myrtle." A myrtle tree in the Bible was often seen as a sign of God's promised blessing or abundance. Esther, the Persian name for Hadassah means "star." Most commonly when we look through the Bible, we see how God raised up a person to lead His people to freedom. But there were also moments where He chooses to manifest His presence to lead them out of captivity. Stay with me here for a minute.

Write Exodus 13:21

Write Matthew 2:9

In these two passages of scripture, we see God manifesting Himself as a cloud by day and a pillar of fire at night or a bright star in the night sky. It's so beautiful that God used Esther like a star, to redeem His people. Esther was created to lead (similar to the star in Matt. 2:9) the people into repentance and restoration to God and bring them out of physical and spiritual captivity. She is part of God's promised blessing to His people. The book of Esther also demonstrates to us how God can use even the most unlikely of our gifts to put us in positions to carry out His purposes.

Let's read Esther 2:7 (NKJV)

"And Mordecai had brought up Hadassah, that is, Esther, his uncle's daughter, for she had neither father nor mother. The young woman was _____ and _____. When her father and mother died, Mordecai took her as his own daughter."

The Hebrew word for lovely as it's used in this passage is defined as, "favorite, loveable, beloved." Favorite is rooted in favor! The kind of favor that results in the restoration of everything the enemy has taken. It was that same kind of favor that crowned her the queen. When describing Esther, it's important to note that verse 7 first points out that she's lovely or favorable and then secondarily beautiful. While it was her beauty at first glance that captured the attention of the King, she only made it into the presence of the king because who she was inside seeped out of her and won her favor with those around her. It was her 'fruit' that made her more beautiful. It was because of this favor that God used her gifts: her beauty, humility, and wisdom to help her people find freedom.

God wants to do the same for us. He wants to use your gifts in the most unique ways to lead others to freedom. When He has a plan for your life, hundreds of others could be in the same arena as you, but your gifts will shine because God will give you favor over that audience. Let's take a look beyond our natural gifts and look at how we need to live our lives so that our gifts can be used to glorify God and point people to Heaven. How do we walk this out? Let's look at what the Word says about living a life that is lovely, filled with humility and wisdom.

> [God] wants to use your gifts in the most unique ways to lead others to freedom.

1. Lovely - Philippians 4:8

"Finally, brethren, whatever things are _____, whatever things are _____, whatever things are just, whatever things are _____, whatever things are _____, whatever things are of good report, if there is any virtue and if there is anything praiseworthy — meditate on these things."

Paul, in this verse, is talking about a lifestyle we are to lead. If we want Jesus to activate our gifts, we need to first live a life that is focused on what is true, noble, pure, and lovely. How do we live in a way that we find favor in all that we do? This means removing yourself from situations or people who desire self-praise rather than seeking to live a life that is praiseworthy to God. It's also taking a good look at our lives to make sure we are living a life that would find favor in the eyes of our Savior. Esther found favor with the king because of how she lived her life, which gave her a voice to rid the kingdom of Haman who was bent on killing the Israelites.

In what areas of your life do you want to be more 'lovely'?

2. Humble - Proverbs 22:4 & 1 Peter 5:6 (NKJV)

"By _____ and the fear of the Lord are riches and honor and life." Proverbs 22:4 (NKJV)

"Therefore _____ yourselves under the mighty hand of God, that He may exalt you in due time..." 1 Peter 5:6 (NKJV)

God is going to use the gifts in your life simply because when He created you, they were weaved into how He formed you. But, there's something supernatural that happens with how God uses those gifts when we humble ourselves before Him and place our trust in Him that He will open the doors for us to use them. Esther's posture of humility made those around her feel seen and known, thus drawing them to her. She could've used her beauty to gain the attention of everyone around her, but her loveliness preceded her, therefore she found favor with everyone amongst those around her, especially the king. That humility allowed her the attention of the king, and granted her favor to come before him without being summoned.

What areas of your life do you feel the Lord convicting you of struggling with pride?

3. Wisdom - Isaiah 11:2 (NKJV)

"The Spirit of the LORD shall rest upon Him, The Spirit of _____ and _____, The Spirit of counsel and might, The Spirit of _____ and of the fear of the LORD."

When Mordecai told Esther Haman's plan to kill all the Jews, we see a defining moment for her. An intersection between these three gifts ultimately led to supernatural favor with the king and freedom for her people. She asks everyone to fast with her for three days so she can prepare. While God isn't mentioned by name, His fingerprints are all over her in this moment. And when she puts on her royal robes and enters the court of the king unannounced, instead of being put to death, the king is delighted to see her. So often we want to run ahead or in circles around God, but His pace never changes. When we move at His pace, we see how loveliness of character, humility, and a desire for wisdom can open up so many more doors for us to use our gifts.

Where do you need wisdom in your life so you can walk in your calling using your gifts?

Diving Deeper

How do you want to see God use your gifts supernaturally? If you could dream up the best day where you're walking in your calling and using your gifts, what would that day look like? Would you be willing to surrender it to God and ask Him to begin to open doors for you?

_____
_____
_____
_____
_____
_____
_____
_____
_____

Neither Esther nor Mordecai had the power or position alone to deliver their people. It was only as they acted in concerted power and authority that they were able to lead God's people through the crisis of death and into deliverance. Neither one of them aspired to the role; perhaps neither of them deserved it. It was thrust on them by a series of improbable circumstances largely beyond their control. Nevertheless, their unlikely partnership accomplished God's ancient promise, and the Jewish race was preserved until, in the fullness of time, God entered history through his people as the messiah. How marvelous are God's inscrutable ways!!

Posture of Prayer

Take some time to pray about those areas of your life where you need to walk in more humility and where you need wisdom. Ask the Lord to begin revealing the areas He wants to help you find healing and breakthrough so that He can use you mightily in your calling, using the firsts He's given you so you can help others find that same healing and freedom.

DAY FIVE

Sadly I've served in many churches over the years where those serving with me have lost their luster for the volunteer positions they've committed to. Between the gossip and the complaints, I found myself getting involved, rather than rising above. The air of complaint seemed like a natural output of doing the serving. I found myself becoming bitter about the "behind the scenes" of a church. We desired to be part of a small church, to truly have the opportunity to get to know the others in the congregation so we could do life together outside of those four walls. This meant that there was always the call from the stage to get involved, the need for people to volunteer and there were never enough people willing to step up. For me, it ended up having the opposite effect and I let the bitterness of others not stepping up drive my reasoning for sitting in service every week. I didn't understand what it looked like to find joy in serving others, I also didn't press through to find a place to serve that allowed me to use all my gifts.

Years later, we found ourselves at a new church. It was the end of July 2020 and we had heard about a church meeting outside in a tent, where people were experiencing radical Holy Spirit transformations and seekers were finding Jesus every single week. From the moment we stepped foot in those tents,

WEEK 4 | UNIQUELY GIFTED

my husband and I looked at each other and said, "we're home." In no time, we were joining the church and learning about all the ways to serve. I couldn't believe how people were lined up excitedly to serve the people of the church. It was contagious! Even our kids wanted to get involved! It didn't take long for us to build relationships and as we did, we started getting calls asking if we would be willing to help out here or there. The difference was this time was people would say, "I see this gift in you and I'm wondering if you'll serve with me, doing ....." I had never been approached that way. So many churches see a need and fill a need, regardless of the giftings that person may carry. Our church desired to see te Holy Spirit use the gifts of His people as they served in the church. Serving in a healthy church makes a huge difference in your Spiritual growth. Serving at our church has opened the doors to leadership opportunities to use gifts that had been dormant within me for so long. But more importantly, it has completely shifted my perspective about what it truly means to serve others.

SEVENTY TIMES SEVEN

Turn in your Bible to 1 Peter 4:10-11. Let's read it together.

"As each has _____ a gift, use it to _____ one another, as good stewards of God's varied grace. Whoever speaks, as one who speaks oracles of God; whoever _____ by the _____ that _____ supplies - in order that in _____ God may be _____ through Jesus Christ. To _____ belong the _____ and dominion forever and ever. Amen." (NKJV)

I even love how The Passion Translations says, "Every believer has received grace gifts, so use them to serve one another as faithful stewards of the many-colored tapestry of God's grace." In the New Testament the Greek word used for grace, according to Strong's Dictionary is charis, which also means favor, pleasure, and thankfulness. It's by God's favor and His pleasure having created you that He's given you such special gifts. Not for you to hoard for your own gain, but for you to use to benefit others. What good is the gift of writing, if you never share your words with others so that they might also hear the Word of God and find Jesus as their Savior? God could find someone else to fill that job because it may seem scary or overwhelming to step into your gifts, but what if He wants to use you?! You, sweet friend, are part of God's many colored tapestry.

Rather, he made himself nothing by taking the very nature of a servant, being made in human likeness.
Philippians 2:7

The word serve appears over 1,100 times in the Bible. In the Old Testament, the Hebrew word for servant 'ebed (eh'-bed)[1], broken down by the Strong's Lexicon as having two key components: action (the servant is a "worker") and obedience. In the New Testament the word is Greek, doulos (doo'-los)[2] which means to be fully dependent, bound to someone, but also one who follows Christ. Even when Christ came, "he made Himself of no reputation, taking the form of a bondservant, and coming in the likeness of man." (Philippians 2:7) Therefore, Christ also calls us to more when we accept Him into our lives. We are no longer slaves to sin, but are bound to becoming righteous (Romans 6:17-18).

Write Matthew 20:26 below

Are you planted in a church? How are you using your gifts within the church to serve others?

As I was praying and preparing for today's study, I felt the Lord put on my heart that there are many of you, like me, who have been part of churches where you felt your gifts were exploited or maybe never utilized. Maybe you served alongside those who led with gossip and complaints. Or for some of you, you wanted to serve but it was so difficult to plug into your church. Those hurts are real. The Lord wants you to know that He sees you and He

---

[1] Gesenius' Hebrew-Chaldee Lexicon, Strong's H5650, "ebed," https://www.blueletterbible.org/lexicon/h5650/kjv/wlc/0-1/
[2] Thayer's Greek Lexicon, Strong's G1401, "doulos," https://www.blueletterbible.org/lexicon/g1401/kjv/tr/0-1/

wants to meet you where you're at right now and lift those hurts from your shoulders. He wants to release you from carrying them so you can walk freely and fully in the charis gifts He's given you. Will you take a moment and lay that hurt at His feet and let Him begin a healing work in you? Oh, friend, I hope you will, I need you to link arms with me to point people to Jesus.

Where has the church hurt you and left you feeling unable to serve?

Let's read Matthew 18:21-35 together.

What does Peter ask Jesus? (Mt. 18:21)

How does Jesus respond to Peter's question? Write Matthew 18:22 in the box below.

Jesus is saying here that forgiveness isn't about the math, it's about the heart. That's why He says seventy times seven, which by the way is 490 times. He knows that it's difficult for us to forgive even one time, let alone forgive repeatedly. The other significance of seventy times seven is that the number seven, Biblically, is the number of completion. When we're willing to sit at the feet of Jesus and offer up forgiveness to those who have hurt us, we find our completion or our wholeness in Him. We have all sinned and fallen short of the glory of God (Rm 8:28), but God offers us a beautiful release from being bound by the hurt others have caused us and that's forgiveness.

Jesus is the ultimate example of what this looks like. When He went to the cross and He died for all of our sins. I don't know about you, but I've walked in sin more than once in my forty-plus years of life. Jesus died not only for my sins and your sins (plural) but the sins of every person He would ever create and would walk this earth. That's a lot more forgiveness than seventy times seven!

How does knowing this about Jesus shift your perspective about the hurt you shared earlier?

Romans 12:9-13 (NKJV)

"Let love be without hypocrisy. Abhor what is evil. Cling to what is good. Be kindly affectionate to one another with brotherly love, in honor giving preference to one another; not lagging in diligence, fervent in spirit, serving the Lord; rejoicing in hope, patient in tribulation, continuing steadfastly in prayer; distributing to the needs of the saints, given to hospitality."

God is calling us to use our gifts to serve others in the body of Christ, but also serve those around us that don't know Jesus, that they would come to know Him by our actions. To walk in this wholeheartedly, we must first forgive, so we no longer walk in the things that once kept us bound. Regardless of how others choose to live their lives. It's like walking in the mud when there's dry ground to the left and the right of you. The mud is thick and as you walk in it, it gets all over your feet, then it splashes up your legs and onto your clothes. Before you know it, it's somehow made its way to your face and in your hair. You feel bogged down and unable to keep walking. God wants to bathe you in His love, and wash you clean, so you can always choose the path on dry ground.

WEEK 4 | UNIQUELY GIFTED

Diving Deeper

What areas of your life are covered in mud? Where have you allowed church hurts to simmer and fester to the point where you are no longer serving using your gifts? What do you feel God is calling you to change so you can be free from this place that has kept you feeling stuck?

_____

_____

_____

_____

_____

_____

_____

I want to end today in Romans 12:2 in The Passion Translation. I know we've talked about this verse in earlier weeks, but that's the beauty of God's Word being living and breathing. There will always be verses that we come back to over and over again because they point the way to being more and more like Jesus so we can be known by Him, walk in our callings, use our gifts--free from what the world wants to place on us to hold us back from experiencing the fullness of what God has for us. I want you to read this over yourself. "Stop imitating the ideals and opinions of the culture around you, be inwardly transformed by the Holy Spirit through a total reformation of how you think. This will empower you to discern God's will as you live a beautiful life, satisfying and perfect in his eyes." Amen!!

Posture of Prayer

Grab your journal and spend the next 10-15 minutes with Jesus. Put on some worship Soaking music and begin to let go of the ways you've allowed past church hurts to keep you from walking in your gifts and serving others, both in and out of those four walls. Talk to Jesus about the magnitude of the forgiveness He freely gave you at the cross, and let go of those hurts! Ask the Lord to forgive you for harboring them for so long and list out person by person if you need to, everyone you need to forgive.

WEEK FIVE

Friends, welcome to week five!

My prayer is that you're finding so much freedom in Jesus, breaking ties with old identities and you're walking into this week feeling lighter. This week we're going to dive into what holds us back from being willing to be used by God in this particular season of our lives? This week, we're going to go deeper into the idea that surrendering in hard seasons to what God is doing, and what He is wanting, is the way to the most beautiful breakthroughs. Abram set an example for us of what it looks like to chase after God and stand on His promises, even when you're walking through unexpected seasons. So did Rahab, Jonah, and other notable women of the Bible who God used for His glory and purposes. Every season requires patience, and only Jesus can supply what we need to wait and walk-through what God knows is best for us.

But as Elizabeth shows us, there is hope in every one of these seasons of patience. It may be a season of learning to experience the joy that comes when we remain in a posture of availability and willingness to be used by God, while simultaneously trusting in His timing. Oh, how I know from personal experience how difficult this is, but I also have experienced the fruit that is produced on our vine as we wait. Whatever God has in store for us, when we go through one of these times in the wilderness, I promise you, breakthrough and breaking forth are the fruit of waiting well, watching and even leaning into the support of others on the journey. If you commit to obedience to God, then you will be amazed at not only where He takes you, but how He gets you there! Let's dive into this week together and see what God has for us!

LIVE BOLDLY IN HIM,

Alissa

group discussion

Take some time to worship together. We have included a worship playlist in the appendix if you need guidance on a song to pick this week.

introduction

Waiting always seems to be a challenge. It's just hard to wait. But, there are different types of waiting. There's waiting for the other shoe to drop. You know that fear of dread of what is coming next. Then, there's waiting with hope and expectation. Don't get me wrong – it's still waiting, but it's hopeful expectation. That's a good kind of waiting.

come together

Open your group with prayer. This should be a brief, simple prayer in which you invite God to be with you as you meet.

Telling our personal stories builds deeper connections among group members. Begin your time together by using the following questions and activities to get people talking. Sharing our stories requires us to be honest. We can help one another be honest and open by creating a safe place; be sure that your group is one where confidentiality is respected, where there is no such thing as "stupid questions," where you listen without criticizing one another.

- How good are you at waiting?

- What thing in your life have you waited for the longest? Has it happened? Are you still waiting?

WEEK 5 | HOPE

watch video session 5
beknownbiblestudy.com/videos

group discussion

grow together

Read Matthew 4:19-20

- How would you have reacted to Jesus invitation to follow Him? Would you have felt prepared to make such a significant decision? Why or why not?

- In the video, Alissa said, "Instead of extracting the beauty in the process, we keep looking to the left and to the right and wondering if there might be a faster way the Lord hasn't thought of to get us there." Why is it difficult at times to find joy in the journey?

- "Our desire to follow Him and chase after Him should always be without delay, but once we're walking with Him, our priority should be to walk at His pace." When do you find yourself trying to run ahead of Jesus' pace? What is the result?

be together

God wants you to be part of His kingdom—to weave your story into His. That will mean change. It will require you to go His way rather than your own. This won't happen overnight, but it should happen steadily.

In this section, talk about how you will apply the wisdom you've learned in this lesson.

- How are trusting and striving related?

- When you feel like your striving in life, where is your level of trust? If you feel like your trusting God, where is your level of striving?

- God's pace never changes. How does your pace change? Why?

- Where are you running ahead of God right now? How is that affecting your level of worry?

- Where are you lagging behind God's pace? What is your reluctance?

- A strong group is made up of people who are all being filled up by Holy Spirit, so that they are empowered to love one another. What commitments will you make to doing the homework each day this week?

- Ask "How can we pray for you this week?" Be sure to write prayer requests in your prayer journal.

Close your meeting with prayer.

WEEK 5

daily study

DAY ONE

I've always loved the story of Jonah and the whale. Only in the Bible would the Lord use a storm and being swallowed by a giant fish to get your attention. Oh, don't get me wrong, the Lord has used plenty of situations to get my attention throughout my life. But I wonder what it would've been like for Jonah to sit in the belly of that whale for three days. The strangest of circumstances led to a beautiful surrendering. For me, it's the breakthrough that comes before the promise that has me chasing after Jesus wholeheartedly. Ways that I've seen God break me wide open and stitch me back up again, leaving no room for me to question His goodness and His faithfulness. Gosh, walking through those moments can be heart-wrenching, and can make you question if this season will ever end. If you will ever feel you're going to be used by God. Yet it's in those same moments I always hear His voice saying, seek me first.

Some of my biggest breakthroughs came after I had my daughter. I was so sure that God was going to give me all boys and I had made peace with that. There were so many insecurities I carried from my childhood into adulthood with me; my biggest fear was passing them on to a girl. Struggles with food, my weight, and my worth. Things that no one would've guessed on the outside, but I had hidden well. When we found out we were pregnant with a girl, I completely panicked. What was I supposed to do with her? I began making a mental checklist of all the things I wouldn't do or say so she never felt the same insecurities as me. As the Lord began to heal me of those insecurities, I realized that I wasn't going to keep her from them by avoidance, but by walking out the healing. It meant acknowledging them as they came up and helping her chase after Jesus to find the same healing I did so she could walk confidently in who God created her to be.

BREAKTHROUGH IN EVERY SEASON

Sweet friend, God has so many plans for your life. I know it can feel as though life has thrown you some unexpected curve balls. Maybe you've struggled in your past, or you're walking through a season right now where you feel like you've been in the wilderness for so long. I used to think that wilderness seasons meant that I had been forgotten by God. He has shown me time and time again that it's in the wilderness where we find His wells of living water. It's there that the Lord prunes off the dead branches and new fruit begins to grow. And from that comes a deeper intimacy with Jesus. It's those seasons that the Lord meets us on our knees, and we learn how to walk in complete surrender to all that He has for us. Yes, it's painful. Yes, it stretches us, but then it strengthens us for what He's calling us to next.

There will always be breakthrough right before the promise!

What is the definition of a breakthrough?

I love this definition so much! Breakthrough means to break forth, break out, burst open. At first glance, it may not look pretty, but the joy that radiates from those who are willing to sit before the Lord and chase after Him makes all the pain, tears, and heartache that led you there worth it. It's wrapped up in His goodness, gentleness, patience, and kindness, that lead us directly into an encounter with the Holy Spirit. When we truly encounter the Holy Spirit, we always leave transformed!

Let's look at Isaiah 58:11 (NKJV) together:

"The Lord will _____ you continually, and _____ your soul in _____ and strengthen your bones; You shall be like a _____ garden, and like a spring of water, whose waters _____ _____ fail."

How beautiful is this verse and the reminder of God's promise? Not only does He guide us, but He longs to be the one to satisfy our souls in when we feel wrung out. To water us like a well-watered garden. Have you ever seen a garden that has been well loved? Every fruit and vegetable are flourishing under the love of its caretaker. Our family had a garden box for a long time in our backyard. It sat under outside our bedroom window. When we built our garden box we researched the best soil to use, what fruit and vegetables would thrive in the different seasons and we set up a drip system. A drip system allows you to set a timer to water all the soil equally at the same time every day. Our garden was well loved. Every day, the kids would excitedly check on our garden to see if the seeds had sprouted. Because we planted them in good soil, tended to them with a good watering system, our garden sprouted quickly and before we knew it, it was producing big and beautiful produce. Just like our garden box, that is how your Heavenly Father cares for you. We get to call upon His strength to get us through whatever season He has us walking in. He longs to water our garden.

God called Abram to pack up everything and set out to a new destination. Not to lush lands with flowing water and fruit, you could pluck from trees as you walked. The land God took him through was the desert. There Abram's faith grew. The Word says he built altars and dug wells. When it came time to part ways with his cousin Lot because their families and the wealth of servants and animals, they had accumulated had grown too big, Abram gave Lot the first choice of the land he wanted to go and settle in. Lot looked to the left and the right, and when he saw the land looked well-watered, he set out towards the east (Genesis 13). We don't see Abram questioning the Lord for taking him out of his homeland to the desert, into a new land, only to have Lot choose the better land for his family. He honors his cousin with the first choice and God's response was, "Look everywhere else. See that land, I'm going to give it to you and your offspring forever."

When have you gone through a season where it felt like you were honoring those around you as they walked in the well-watered land, yet you felt you were still in the desert?

How have you continued to worship God in those seasons?

The Lord desires for us to chase after him in the peaks and the valleys. It's easy to give all our worship to Jesus when things are going amazing in our lives. Where we feel blessing and favor everywhere we turn. It's when we're struggling, that we begin to take control. I promise you and I cannot steer the ship as well as God can. True, vulnerable, face planted to the floor worship is what brings the breakthrough. It may not be immediate. It may happen a little at a time, but it's for our healing. It's the cracking open, emptying ourselves out that gives the Holy Spirit permission to seep into the deepest parts of our souls and put us back together.

Today we're going to look at another woman who could've been forever defined by how she had lived her life. She could've carried the name and the occupation so many had given her but saving the lives of two spies Joshua had sent on a mission to Jericho and an encounter with God, changed the entire trajectory of her life.

Let's read Joshua 2 together.

What is Rahab known for in the city of Jericho? _____

When the men sent from the King of Jericho come knocking on her door, where does Rahab say the men are? Where are they?

Joshua had sent spies to Jericho to scout the city and the land because he knew God had promised them the land. When the men enter the city looking for a place to stay, they're referred to the home of Rahab. The place is known for the comings and goings of nomadic men, traveling in and out of the city. Yet, Rahab recognizes them as Israelite men and instead of turning them in, she hides them under the stalks of flax she had laid out on her rooftop. When the king's men come, she lies and tells them the men have already left before the city doors close.

Sometimes as God's refining us out of one season and into the next, we're still learning to turn from our old sinful ways. Rahab lived her life as a prostitute, running a home for men to come and go from her bed. By others, she had been labeled a harlot. She might've saved the lives of those men that night, but God saves hers, and through her, the lives of her family members. She asks the men to show kindness to her family when they come to destroy the city of Jericho. Kindness, as it's used in this reference, translates as the Hebrew word hesed[3] which means to show "mercy" or "love." Essentially, she's asking these men if God will show love and mercy towards her and save her and her family from destruction. Not only does God save Rahab and her family from death that day, but He redeems her life!

Write Hebrews 11:31

Rahab goes from being known as a Harlot to being saved by God and living among the Israelites. She marries a man named Salmon, and gives birth to a son Boaz, who will one day honor a woman's reputation so no one mistakes her for a harlot. Wow! It's just so beautiful how the Lord's greatest desire is to redeem us from our past, wipe the slate clean and bless us in ways that are even beyond our comprehension.

Maybe you've known Jesus for a long time, but you're still struggling to let go of some things from your past and they're keeping you in a season of feeling as though you cannot be used by God. Friend, that couldn't be farther from the truth. I believe that God's knocking at the door of your heart, will you let Him in to do that healing work so you can break free, burst forth, and leave it behind? Rahab might've been known at one time as a prostitute, but God transformed her life so radically that she then becomes known as one of the five women mentioned in the line of Jesus. Hallelujah! God has that same plan for your life.

---

[3] Gesenius' Hebrew-Chaldee Lexion, Strong's H2617, "Hesed"

WEEK 5 | HOPE

Diving Deeper

What areas of your life have you allowed your season, past or present to name you, define you or keep you from walking in a deeper relationship with Jesus? How has the Lord been stirring in your heart today to let it go? Are you willing to allow Him to give you breakthroughs in those areas today?

_____
_____
_____
_____
_____
_____
_____
_____
_____

It's so easy to subscribe to the belief that God can't use me because…. You fill in the blank. I promise that can't be further from the truth. God often uses our healing to bring breakthroughs for others. Your seasons don't define you, He does. Ecclesiastes 3:1 reminds us, "To everything there is a season, A time for every purpose under heaven." Our relationship with the Lord grows, bringing deeper intimacy and an increase in faith when we are willing to ask Him what He is trying to teach us in every season we are in. Is He refining you? Healing you? Commanding you to step out boldly in faith? Just remember, it's never to sit you on the bench.

> There is a time for everything, and a season for every activity under the heavens.
> *Ecclesiastes 3:1*

Posture of Prayer

Spend some time today journaling and praying to release the burdens you've been carrying. Tell Him about the season you've been walking in and begin to declare scripture over the promises He has for your life. Even if you don't know what they are yet, still spend time declaring them. I promise if you do, the Lord will meet you right where you are at. Breakthrough is imminent when we're willing to lay it all at His feet.

(BE) KNOWN

DAY TWO

Of all the fruit of the spirit, patience has always been one I've struggled with. I'd like to blame it on my Type A personality, but I have a feeling I'm not the only one who struggles with this, regardless of our personality type. Maybe that's why there are so many verses about patience in the Bible or the way we see it as a constant underlying theme throughout God's Word. Have you ever read the Bible from Genesis to Revelation? If you haven't, I fully recommend it. There's nothing like reading the Word from beginning to end and seeing the overarching themes God shows you. In January of this year, God prompted me to read the entire Bible in 30 days. Yes, you read that right, Genesis 1 to Revelation 22. Between reading and listening to it on the Bible app in the plan I was following, I was in the Word for almost three hours a day, separate from my quiet time. Reading that quickly was incredible, but it was like a fire hose that didn't turn off. Looking back, the Lord showed me many themes as I read, but the biggest two were: there is a beauty that comes from patience. I caught many overarching themes and promises, but it gave me a thirst for going back and reading it again, more slowly. The second thing the Lord showed me was how He blessed those who were obedient in every season.

January is a season of time in and of itself. Straight off the holidays, we're all making goals, vision boards, cracking open new paper planners, making to-do's, and gearing up for the final months before summer. I wasn't doing any of that. My only plan was to complete the 30-day "shred" and spend as much time in the Word as possible. Looking back, I have no idea where those extra hours came from, but they gave me a desire to be more intentional with the time I spent with Jesus. To weave patience into my quiet times with Him in the morning. To set the table for our time together. I moved my quiet time to the dining room table, set up my Bible, notebook, prayer journal, and a candle the night before, and found myself setting my alarm for earlier and earlier so I didn't need to rush my time in His presence. When I began to slow down, the Lord began to move. He put this Bible study in my heart, and I began writing. Even amid pitching the book to agents and publishers. Our time with the Lord is never wasted. It doesn't matter what season we find ourselves in, there's never one He's not waiting to meet us in. I don't know about you, but I'm so thankful for that!

PATIENCE IN EVERY SEASON

As I was studying for this week, I felt the Lord impress upon my heart, a desire for us to understand and acknowledge that we're all going to experience different seasons in our lives. Some of them will leave us feeling elated; others will have us questioning how we will see God in the midst of it. No matter the season, Jesus wants us to look at the posture of our hearts and how we are to seek Him during every season we find ourselves in. God never brings us through peaks and valleys without desiring to draw us closer to Him. When we can chase after Him in the valleys when we cannot see what is around the next bend in the road, we will chase Him on the highest hilltops. He will help us dig our wells so that He can quench our thirst with His living water. The rest of this week we're going to be looking at how we are to respond to seasons of waiting. We're going to dive deep into the Word and and talk about how we should posture ourselves before the Lord in every season. How do we find our patience, hope, and joy?

Finding patience, hope, and joy boils down to one thing: understanding God's timing for every season. Here's the beautiful thing about Jesus — no matter what pace you're trying to run, His never changes. Never increases or decreases, always patiently waiting for you to circle back and join Him. Patience in every season means learning how to walk with Him, at His pace and learn all He's trying to teach you.

Let's read Acts 1:1-12 together.

After the resurrection of Jesus, He appeared to people for forty days, preaching, teaching, and sharing meals with them. The disciples who had scattered at His crucifixion have all made their way back together and are traveling with Jesus. I'm overwhelmed just thinking about what these 40 days would've been like. Jesus, sent to earth in human form, went to the cross, suffered humiliation, and died a brutal death. He was the ultimate sacrifice that we would have direct access to God. We see Jesus' patience to teach His disciples, and patience with the people who questioned and rebuked Him, and patience to begin His ministry (He was 30 before His ministry began).

What did Jesus do in the forty days after His resurrection? (vs 3-4)

Psalm 27:14

Rather than wiping His hands and declaring His work on earth done when He rose from the dead, Jesus spends the next forty days showing Himself to the disciples and others. Offering proof of His resurrection, redemption, and forgiveness and patiently teaching them how to live without Him once He has ascended to Heaven. The difference is, this time, the disciples fully understood what He had been trying to tell them all along. He might be leaving them physically, but He will send a gift in His place. The gift of the Holy Spirit who gives us power and authority to be the hands and feet of Jesus while we're here on earth.

As we dive into how we are emboldened by living in a posture of patience in each season we're in, let's go back to the Old Testament and look at a beautiful trail of verses that will lead us back to Acts 1.

Write Psalm 27:14 in the margin.

WEEK 5 | HOPE

David is writing this Psalm to God in a season where his future is unknown. He is asking the Lord to bring him victory against all those who are conspiring against him, while simultaneously acknowledging that the Lord is his foundation, and he will seek Him all the days of his life. When we reach verse 14, David's prayer declares he will wait for the Lord. In this moment he knows being patient is not an easy task, which is why we see him say it twice in the same verse. Anytime we see words or phrases repeated close together, we want to sit up and take notice.

If we follow the beautiful trail of crumbs God so graciously leads us, Psalm 27:14 has several coinciding verses giving us a glimpse into what happens when we wait on the Lord. Let's dive in together, shall we?

> Verse fourteen took me to Psalm 33:20, which says, "We _____ in hope for the Lord; he is our help and our shield."

> Then Psalm 130:5-6, "I _____ for the Lord, my soul _____ and in his word I put my hope. My soul _____ for the Lord more than watchman _____ for the morning.

> From there, let's turn to Isaiah 8:17, "I will _____ for the Lord, who is hiding his face from the house of Jacob. I will put my trust in Him.

Isn't it beautiful how scripture is already tying this into a bow for us? Stay with me I have a couple more verses for us to look at.

> Isaiah 30:18, "Yet the Lord longs to be gracious to you; he rises to show you compassion. For the Lord is a God of justice. Blessed are all who _____ for Him.

> Isaiah 30:18 takes us to Habakkuk 2:3 which says, "For the revelation _____ an appointed time, it speaks of the end and will to prove false. Though it lingers, _____ for it; it will certainly come and not delay."

And what do you know, at the end of our trail of breadcrumbs we land back in Acts 1:4. God is so good! Let's write it below.

Looking at all of these scriptures, what do we receive from God when we live in a posture of patience in every season we find ourselves in? Glance back at the verses we just studied to help you find your answers.

Now it's your turn. Look up a verse that talks about waiting or patience and write it below.

When we choose to exercise the fruit of patience in our life, God helps us, protects us, gives us hope, and is gracious and compassionate towards us. And He gives us the Holy Spirit as a guide. The disciples had followed Jesus for three years, yet in those forty days after He was resurrected and walked with them, everything He spoke about during His active ministry, they finally grasped it. That's why when Jesus told them to go to Jerusalem and wait in the upper room for the gift He wanted to give them, they went. In that upper room, they prayed, worshiped, and waited because they knew the gift Jesus would give them would be every bit worth the wait.

If you want to, I encourage you to read ahead to Acts 2. On the day of Pentecost, when the 120 who stayed in the upper room received the full power and anointing of the Holy Spirit. What it must've been like to see God's glory fall and all those men and women receive the gift of Jesus' promise because they chose to wait on Him!

Tomorrow we're going to dive into what it looks like to have a posture of hope in every season. I can't wait and I hope you're excited too.

WEEK 5 | HOPE

Diving Deeper

Looking back at the scriptures we read today, which one spoke to your heart the most today? What gift could you use right now to help you live in a posture of patience? What does the season you're in look like?

_____
_____
_____
_____
_____
_____
_____
_____
_____
_____
_____
_____
_____

Praise Jesus that even as we wait, we already have access to the power and anointing of the Holy Spirit. He is our strength and our guide, helping us to live out the fruit of the Spirit and patiently wait on the Lord for where He wants to lead us next. Don't run ahead of Jesus, there is an abundance of blessing waiting for you by His side.

Posture of Prayer

Spend some time journaling and asking the Lord what areas He's asking you to patiently wait on Him in this season. Acknowledge the gifts we receive by waiting and spending some time thanking Him, and also asking Him to begin to show you what is coming.

DAY THREE

I remember when we found out we were pregnant with our first child. On our third anniversary, we began talking and dreaming about what it would be like to begin our family. Five weeks later we looked down and two bright pink lines stared back at us. I think we just stared at each other, completely excited and scared out of our minds. It never occurred to us that we would conceive so fast. We told friends and family right at six weeks before there were signs of a bump or a heartbeat. Then we waited. No one prepares you for the ten months of pregnancy waiting and anticipation. I found myself making a wish list of hopes for our first child. Beginning with the hope of an easy, pain-free delivery. Oh, how young and naive I was! Then came the hope that nursing would be a breeze. Easy latching, skin-to-skin bonding time where we would sit for hours staring into each other's eyes. The list went on and on. Now looking back, I realized there was one hope that was missing from my list and that was the hope that God would show us how to tether our child to Him as she grew.

Our delivery turned into an emergency c-section where our sweet girl's heart rate dropped dangerously low. The pumping of drugs so quickly into my system made my body wracked with tremors. There was a team of what felt like 20 people in the delivery room with my husband and me, one for every emergency service she could possibly need. They put her on my chest for a split second once they determined her vitals stable and then wheeled her off, *my husband in tow while I laid there in the operating room being stitched back together. There were so many tears. I felt like the delivery was an out-of-body experience. As I looked around the room, instead of grieving what I had lost, I began seeing the hope of being there that night. Her heart rate dropped close to midnight, and no one was delivering at that time, so the OR was open, the anesthesiologist was ready, my doctor and the entire team needed to assist weren't tied up in another room and my husband was with me and when they needed to take our sweet girl for more tests, he was able to go with her, so she was never alone. We don't always understand why our seasons aren't finely paved roads with no potholes, seventy-degree sunny weather with a breeze, but we know there's never an absence of hope that comes from being bound to Jesus.*

HOPE IN EVERY SEASON

Let's take a moment to look up the meaning of the word, 'hope':

Yes, hope is a feeling of expectation - a desire for something certain to happen, but listed right below it is the word, trust. When we put our hope in Jesus, we are saying, we trust you. No matter what the circumstances, even if we're not sure of the outcome, we know You are in control and we will hope for the fulfillment of His promises in our life. According to Strong's Concordance, there are two words the Hebrew language uses for the word Hope. One is the word "Tikva" (tik-vaw')[4] and the other is "Yahal." (yaw-chal')[5]. Tikva means, "cord (to bind), or expectation," and Yahal means, "hope or to wait." Did you know that the first instance we see of someone binding a cord (scarlet) and putting her hope in God as she waited to be saved from the destruction of her city is Rahab? How good is God?! I didn't even put this all together till I began studying in preparation for today. On day one of this week, we talked about Rahab and what it means to not be defined by our circumstances. Here she is joining us again as we talk today about having hope. God's Word is alive and so beautiful, don't you agree? I love it when I find Biblical connections like this; it makes me so excited! I'm learning right beside all of you!

---

[4] Gesenius' Hebrew-Chaldee Lexicon, Strong's H8614, "Tikva"

[5] Gesenius' Hebrew- Chaldee Lexicon, Strongs H3176, "Yahal"

We cannot have patience without having hope for how God is going to bring us through this season.

Hope is rooted in the waiting. We cannot have patience without having hope for how God is going to bring us through this season. God is a good God. He desires to bless His children. That includes you and me, friend. You are a daughter of the most high King, heir to His throne. This world is temporary, but we live in the hope of what we know is waiting for us in heaven. As we hope for what we will someday get to enjoy, how are we demonstrating that hope while we are still here on earth that others may come to know Jesus through our example?

When is a time you've had to "bind yourself in hope" to God? How did you experience Him during that time?

Write Hebrews 6:19 below:

An anchor is bound to a cord, which is secured to the boat. The anchor is steadfast. It allows the boat to move in the water, but never go far from where it is tethered to the ocean floor. It grounds the boat, so it can become a safe place for people to enjoy each other, the water, and the waves. We fully experience the hope that the boat will not move far from the tethering point because it's securely anchored. Do you see Jesus as someone you can anchor your hope in? I won't make you answer that now, but I encourage you to spend some time thinking about how you would respond. To anchor your hope in Jesus means you have to trust Him. Sometimes, in certain seasons that's easier said than done. I'm speaking to myself on this one too.

Write Jeremiah 17:7 (NKJV)

"Blessed is the man who _____ in the Lord, and whose _____ is in the Lord."

Today we're going to read about two exceptionally beautiful women inside and out, who bound themselves together and put their hope in God and each other to get them through a devastating season of loss.

Let's read Ruth 1:1-22.

As you read the passage, underline the word hope wherever you see it.

In this passage, we see one instance where Naomi uses the word, hope. In verses 12-13a she says, "Turn back, my daughters, go—for I am too old to have a husband. If I should say I have hope, if I should have a husband tonight and should also bear sons, would you wait for them till they were grown?" Can you feel the agony in her voice as she reaches for hope? Even if she could hope for a husband and more sons, would they truly wait for them to be grown? Her hopes for what her future would look like change in the blink of an eye when her husband and sons pass away. Naomi is now going to make the journey back to her homeland and hopes that one of her extended family members will take her in and care for her. She's balancing a tightrope between hope and hopelessness as she sends her daughter in laws home to their families. Isn't that the same tightrope we walk on when we walk through unexpected seasons?

How does Ruth respond? Write Ruth 1:16 below

Ruth chooses to bind herself to Naomi. "Your people will be my people, your God my God." What a beautiful expression of hope for what the future can bring. She sees evidence of Naomi's faith in God. In a moment when she could return to her family and her gods, she places her hope in Naomi's God to take care of them as they return to the land of Naomi's family.

How do you think Naomi is feeling at that moment? How about Ruth?

Possibly expectation in the waiting. Hope. That's what it looks like. Taking God's hand, placing all our trust in Him, in every season we find ourselves in Then waiting with expectation for what He is going to do and the promises He is going to fulfill. If you're going through a season of waiting and you need to find hope, I want to encourage you to chase after Jesus. Begin to read and declare scripture over your life. Below are some of my favorites that point to what we receive when we find our hope in our Heavenly Father.

You will be blessed, Psalm 146:5, "Blessed is he whose help is the God of Jacob, whose _____ is in the Lord his God."

God is your portion, Lamentations 3:24, "The Lord is my portion, says my soul, therefore I _____ in Him."

God won't disappoint you, Romans 5:5, "Now _____ does not disappoint because the love of God has been poured out in our hearts by the Holy Spirit who was given to us."

Brings perseverance, Romans 8:25, "but we have _____ for what we do not see, we eagerly wait for it with perseverance."

Gives us joy and peace, Romans 15:13, "Now my the God of _____ fill you with all joy and peace in believing that you may abound in _____ by the power of the Holy Spirit."

See God's faithfulness, Hebrews 10:23, "Let us hold fast to the confession of _____ without wavering, for the one who has promised is faithful."

Which one of these scriptures do you need to lean on for hope in this season?

Diving Deeper

How do you see Jesus as someone you can anchor your hope in? If you don't see Him that way because you feel He's let you down in the past, I want to encourage you that God is not a God of disappointment. Take a few minutes to journal ways you want to see Jesus as someone you can anchor your hope in and begin asking Him to show you how to do that. Share a time you found your hope in Jesus, what happened and what fruit did it produce in your life?

_____
_____
_____
_____
_____
_____

There is fruit when we put our HOPE in Jesus! Just declaring these scriptures over us takes captive any thoughts of the enemy that we can't be used by God in every season we're in. It's so easy to think we're only used when we're producing good social media content, writing a book, or standing on stage, but the truth is our greatest calling begins in our home. The fruit that is produced in private will always come to light in the open.

Posture of Prayer

Take some time to journal what the Lord spoke to you about hope in your season today. How were you encouraged? Where are you struggling to trust Jesus? Spend some time surrendering trust back to Him and committing to finding hope in Him.

(BE)KNOWN

DAY FOUR

Have you ever found a scripture that sits on your heart so heavy? One that the Lord continuously pops into your head. At the beginning of 2022, I was working on co-writing a small group curriculum with a friend. We felt the Lord tug so strongly on our hearts that we were to take our small group through a study of Romans 12. I don't know if you've ever spent time studying that chapter, but it truly is a lighthouse for how, as believers, we are called to live as disciples of Jesus. The entire chapter is beautiful and challenging, but verse ten has stuck with me. It has completely challenged and changed my perspective on how we are to live in every season. "Be devoted to one another in love. Honor one another above yourselves." Depending on the translation you're reading from, it might include, "giving preference to honoring" or "outdo." In this context, the word honor means to literally value that person, go before, or lead the way with genuine recognition.

As the Lord and I have walked this journey of obedience to study His Word and write, there have been so many moments where I've had friends who started after me or never thought they would write a book, and sign with agents and publishers. I won't lie, it has challenged me. It has made me question if I heard the Lord right because some of those women have been teaching and leading others in the Word a lot longer than me, making them more qualified in my mind. I can't tell you how many times

I've asked the Lord for confirmation I was still walking on His path and surrendering this dream to Him. During it all, I found myself seeing this verse like ticker tape across my heart, "outdo yourselves in respect and honoring of one another" (TPT). The outpouring of that honor is a joy! I found so much joy in supporting my girlfriends and being a cheerleader in their corner for the books they were writing. I love that the Lord is putting it on the heart of so many women to go out and teach His Word! It's been an honor to link arms with them on their journeys!

JOY IN EVERY SEASON

Today we're going to look at the posture of joy in every season. Joy: a word associated with happiness or excitement is often confused with an emotion that comes and goes based on what is happening in our lives. Yet the Bible talks about joy as a choice. It talks about a state of being regardless of what we're walking through. Gosh, some days that just seems so overwhelming. That's why it's so important that we're chasing after a deeper intimacy with Jesus, creating that secret place where we read His Word and pray so we can hide it in our hearts. Then when we walk through seasons that make us start comparing our lives to others, we can stand in the joy that comes from serving a good God and knows that He has a plan for each of us as well.

I'm so excited for today! There is no doubt in my mind that God has great plans for your life! I can't wait to link arms with you as you begin to move into a season of activation. One of the reasons I felt the Lord impress this Bible study and book on my heart was because His greatest desire is for His daughters to know Him deeper. So, we could stand firm on our identity in Him, and begin to allow Him to give us new dreams and visions where He can use our gifts and talents to glorify Him no matter what season we're in. When we can stand on scriptural truth, but also allow Him to come in and do the transformational work, then we can stand together, arm in arm, free of comparison, counting it all as joy that we get to walk this road together. If it takes more than one person to build a house, it takes all of us to build the kingdom.

Who are some women in your life that you've linked arms?

What fruit displayed in their lives drew you to walk with them?

Turn with me to Philippians 2:2-3.

"Fulfill my _____ by being _____, having the same love, being of _____ accord and _____ mind. Let _____ be done through selfish ambition or conceit, but in the _____ of mind each _____ others better than himself." (NKJV)

The Passion Translation says, "walk together with one harmonious purpose and you will fill my heart with unbounded joy." Paul isn't telling us to walk this out with some people, or only people we know, like, or feel comfortable with. He's telling us to walk this out with everyone. We don't get to pick and choose the person or the situation, we are called to be joined in perfect unity with all women and the result of that is bringing God unbounded joy!

Write Habakkuk 3:18 below:

In what areas of your life do you compare yourself to others?

Why do you think women find it hard to honor women around them?

I'd like to challenge us all today to spend some time at the Lord's feet, sweeping out those areas of our lives where we've fallen into the comparison trap. Where we've let envy fester. And we've begun to distrust the calling God has put on our lives. Remember, in every season God brings us through, He's also working in us to bring us breakthroughs in those areas. Where He wants to take you, He knows you won't have time to hold onto these feelings, so let's choose joy and let them go.

Today we're going to land in Luke chapter one, with two faith-filled women, in two different seasons of life, both choosing joy amid their circumstances, and we will watch how they link arms and honor one another.

Read Luke 1:39-56

Who are the two women we're studying today and how do they know each other?

What does Elizabeth's name mean? _____

What does Mary's name mean? _____

Let's add them both to our chart on page 236. Earlier in Luke chapter one, we see an angel of the Lord appear to Elizabeth's husband Zechariah and tell him that his wife would give birth to a baby boy. The Bible says they are both "well along in age," and Elizabeth had been barren, unable to have children. We don't know how well along in age is defined, but some scholars believe she was in her sixties. While this news was hard for Zechariah to swallow, the moment Elizabeth finds out she was pregnant, she goes into seclusion for five months. When we reach the gospels, it's the first time we see any sign of God and prophecy in 400 years. God had been silent! Yet, Elizabeth still trusted God, she sought a relationship with God and when she found out she's pregnant as the angel of the Lord prophesied, she went into her secret place to worship Him. I don't know about you but if I found myself pregnant after years of chasing after God in desperation for a child, I would be shouting from the rooftops. Elizabeth dug deeper into God's presence.

At the same time this is happening, hundreds of miles away, her sweet little cousin Mary gets betrothed to a man named Joseph. An angel of the Lord appears to her and tells her she will carry the son of God. Mary is in her late teens, probably between sixteen and eighteen when she becomes pregnant. We've all seen first-hand in the twenty-first century what the stigma of pregnancy out of wedlock can do, imagine for a moment what it looked like for Mary. In the middle of her and Joseph navigating being unmarried and now the to be parents of the son of God, Mary finds out from an angel of the Lord that her cousin Elizabeth is six months pregnant, and she immediately goes to her.

What happens when these two pregnant women see each other (vs 41)?

Two women, one in her teen years, one in her sixties, both pregnant with men that are going to change the world. One barren almost all her life and another unmarried and pregnant. Yet... when they come together there is no comparison, no judgment, there is nothing but joy and honor and a shared feeling of God's blessing and favor over their lives. It would've been so easy for Elizabeth to feel that Mary's visit was meant to steal the spotlight of her pregnancy.

What does Elizabeth say in verse 45?

Write Acts 2:28.

Maybe you're already in a season where you've seen the fruit that comes from the breakthrough, the hope, and the joy. You've been patient and you're beginning to see the Lord open doors you've been praying to walk through. Have you asked the Lord if there's a woman in your life that is clinging to that promise, some days through tears, that He wants you to encourage? We are called to build each other's faith. We do that by living in the opposite vein of the world. Where the world pits women against each other, the women of the church are called to unify. We were created to be builders!!

WEEK 5 | HOPE

Diving Deeper

Do you struggle with comparison? How has it stolen your joy? How is what we studied today about honoring one another challenging you to look at your relationships with other women differently?

_____

_____

_____

_____

_____

Jeremiah 17:7-8 says, "Blessed is the man who trusts in the Lord. Whose confidence is in him. He will be like a tree planted by the water that sends out its roots by the stream. It does not fear when heat comes; its leaves are always green. It has no worries in a year of doubt and it never fails to bear fruit." This is such a beautiful picture of what we look like when we wait patiently on the Lord, put our hope in the promises He's spoken over us, and we live a life of joy, regardless of the season we're walking it. Why? Because we know that God is good, and we can walk on His promises!

Posture of Prayer

Spend some time journaling and thanking the Lord for the fruit of the Spirit and ask Him to bear those fruit in your life. Repent if there are women in your life, you've struggled to honor and support as they've walked in what God has called them to. Ask Him for the courage to link arms with the woman on either side of you and chase after building the kingdom together.

DAY FIVE

I remember when I began blogging in 2007. It was towards the beginning of this era of online journaling. Newly pregnant, and teaching full-time while finishing my Master's degree, I was looking for an outlet and a way to document my pregnancy. One blog post turned into many, which led to teaching myself how to sew and opening an Etsy shop. As the blog began to grow, brands began reaching out to me asking if I would partner with them to talk about their products. Cost Plus World Market was my first client. After months of paid partnerships, they hired me to find other bloggers, like myself, to work with. That was the birth of Pollinate Media Group. A matchmaker between brands and bloggers to create authentic, evergreen content that would create brand awareness and loyalty for consumers. Over the next twelve years, we worked with hundreds of brands and thousands of bloggers and I've had the privilege of working alongside some amazing women who worked on the Pollinate team behind the scenes with me.

In 2019 the Lord began stirring in my heart the promise of more. I had no idea what that meant, but I felt the shift in my spirit. In May of that year, the Lord gave me the title for my book and an outline of the chapters in my quiet time one morning. I wrote it down obediently and spent the next year sharing with the Lord all the reasons He should choose someone else. In the back and forth with the

Lord, I found myself in His Word more and more and couldn't shake that Pollinate was something beautiful, birthed out of obedience and blessing, but that the Lord had more. One morning in early 2020 He asked me if I would be willing to let it go. "Absolutely not," was my initial response. He would ask me morning after morning until I realized my identity was more wrapped up in my company than Him. That morning I laid it at His feet and said, if He took it away, I would be willing to let it go because I knew He had something better for my life. A month later covid hit, everything shut down, marketing budgets changed and for many months none of my clients ran influencer marketing programs. I began meeting with the Lord every morning, reading His word, journaling prayers, and writing... willingly and obediently.

A POSTURE OF WILLINGNESS

On day one we talked about how each season leads to a breakthrough and a promise. That only comes with a willingness to seek Jesus in a new and deeper way. When we choose to press in even when we feel as if we're going through a pressing. How do we do this? Through our posture in each season. Then we talked about what that posture looks like. We wait on the Lord, we hope in the Lord, and we choose to find joy in the Lord, in every season we walk through because we know it all leads to a deeper intimacy with Him. If you look at all the men and women in the Bible we've studied over the last five weeks, we see how they all experienced the fullness of God's promise for their lives because of their willingness to surrender and simply answer the call to come. Because He cares, and there is more.

What is the definition of willing?

So often we're so busy being full of our own plans, our own goals, and fulfilling our own desires that we want God to bless our lives and businesses, but we don't trust Him to be in the details. We don't want to relinquish control. Yet, the Bible talks about having a willing heart, which means to be "forward in spirit, predisposed, ready and willing." It's a posture of, "yes I will...." Even if it's hard. Even if I have to walk through unknown territory. Even if there are moments of loneliness.

I will wait. I will keep my hope in you and trust that what you have for me is good. I will choose joy in the midst of it all.

Write Genesis 2:18

In the beginning of time, God said, it is not good for man to be alone, I will make a helper for Him. We see a repeated pattern of God bringing a helper, so we never have to walk alone. God manifested Himself through burning bushes, a staff turning into a snake, water coming from rocks, large bodies of water parting, angels of the Lord visiting, a bright star in the sky, and then His only son, who came and died willingly for our sin and rose again three days later. Then, after all of that, Jesus gave us the gift of the Holy Spirit to live inside of us and help comfort us, guide us, and help us live seeped in the fruit of the spirit.

With willingness comes obedience. When I say the word obey, what is your immediate response? Why is that?

Write Micah 7:7 from the NKJV below:

The word "will" appears three times in this verse. Whenever we see a word repeated more than once, especially in the same verse, it's worth taking a closer look to see what the author is emphasizing.

WEEK 5 | HOPE

- The first time we see the word "will" is at the beginning of the verse where it says, "I will look." According to Strong's Lexicon, "will" translated to Hebrew is "sapa" (tsaw-faw)[6] stemming from a simple action which means to lean forward, and look out. It doesn't signify an event that happens one time, but a repeated action on our part.

- In the second instance "I will wait," "will" is the Hebrew word yahal (yaw-chal)[7], which means to hope, wait, remain, or delay. To live a life that is willing to come to the feet of Jesus in a posture of surrender, knowing that God is good, all the time, in every season.

- The final use of this word is in the phrase, "will hear me." "Will"l in this case is the Hebrew word, "sama" (shaw-mah)[8], which means to hear, listen or understand and obey. When we're willing to listen and obey, God will speak to us and He will use us. He's looking for a willing heart.

What do we learn from these three definitions of "will" that show the Lord that we are willing to be used by Him, however, He chooses to use us, in every season we find ourselves in?

Which one of these three "I will's" is most difficult for you:

Read Exodus 4:10-17

What reasoning does Moses give God for why he can't lead the Israelites (vs 10)?

What does God remind Moses (vs 11)?

---

[6] Gesenius' Hebrew-Chaldee Lexicon, Strong's H6822, "sapa"
[7] Gesenius' Hewbew-Chaldee Lexicon, Strong's H3176, "yahal"
[8] Gesenius' Hebrew- Chaldee Lexicon, Strong's H8085, "sama"

Write Exodus 4:12

When God calls us and we approach His throne with a willingness to be used to build the kingdom, we don't need to have all the tools to accomplish it. We just need to be willing to walk through the breakthrough, stay in a posture of patience, place our hope in Jesus, and choose joy, always standing on the assurance that if He has promised it, He will do it.

- Peter willingly stepped out on the water when Jesus said come, he stood on God's promise to protect him.

- Mary willingly sat at Jesus' feet every time she saw Him because she understood the promise that He would never leave her.

- Deborah willingly sought God in the secret place, always waiting and seeking His guidance with a willing heart to take care of the Israelites as a mother would her children.

- The woman at the well willingly left her bucket at the well after she encountered Jesus so that she could tell others about what He could do for them too.

- Esther willingly fasted, prayed, and prepared to enter the king's court without being summoned to free the Israelites from captivity.

- Ruth willingly left her homeland and her family because of her deep love for her mother-in-law Naomi and a desire to stay with her and take care of her.

- Jesus willingly went to the cross and died for every single one of our sins and those who came before us and after us so we would have direct access to God. Then He willingly gave us the gift of the Holy Spirit to guide us.

Diving Deeper

What holds you back from being willing to be used by God in this season? Why do you believe you've allowed this to be an area of stronghold in your life? Are you willing to surrender it now?

_____
_____
_____
_____
_____
_____
_____
_____
_____
_____

Each of us is invited into a deeper relationship with Jesus regardless of where we begin. There is always more for every one of us. My prayer as you wrap up this week is that the Lord spoke to your heart, confirming the stirrings and the promises He has declared over you. It all begins with breakthrough, posture, and a willing heart. Praise Jesus we serve a God who begins with using those with those who are willing to serve others and build His kingdom!

Posture of Prayer

Spend some time talking to God about what has kept you from feeling like you can be used to build His kingdom in this season. Maybe you need to let go of a past disappointment, or maybe you feel like Moses and his stutter, and you see it as a problem or hindrance rather than a strength. Leave it all at Jesus' feet and spend some time waiting for Him to lavish His presence over you and fill those areas of your life with a strength that only comes from Him to go out and walk confidently on His promises for your life.

WEEK SIX

I can hardly believe we're almost done!

I pray that God has done more in you in these six weeks than you ever imagined that He could! In this final week of being known, we are going to dive deeper into the idea of being about the business of our Father in heaven in the same way that Jesus was.

He came full stop for our salvation. Saving sinners is what His Father sent Him to do. But while He was here, He also built the seeds of His Church, and He called His followers to be empowered to do the same things He did. Jesus wants to be just a prayer away from us so that He can partner with us as we walk in obedience to Him and His calling on our life. We'll talk about prayer this week as a major way we serve others.

We'll also look again at a crucial aspect of Jesus' ministry. Everything He did as He walked on earth was born out of who He knew Himself to be. Jesus longs for us to know who we are IN HIM, as we walk the road He calls us to travel. And He never asks us to travel a road He Himself has not traveled first. The greatest news is that wherever He sends us, He comes along with us.

As we go through this last week together, have confidence in who He's called you to be. Consider what He may be asking you to give over to Him so that He can fill those places with Himself. How awesome is it to BE KNOWN by Jesus, to be sent by Jesus to wash the feet of others, and walk in the breakthrough of freedom that comes from knowing who we are in Him?! One more week! Praying that the Lord meets you in a fresh and beautiful way this week as we close out our time together.

LIVE BOLDLY IN HIM,

Alisa

group discussion

Take some time to worship together. We have included a worship playlist in the appendix if you need guidance on a song to pick this week.

introduction

How's your confidence? Do you boldly ask or do you hesitate? Do you plunge in or do you hold back? There are times for caution, but there are also times for action. Confidence plays a big part in moving forward in the things of God. This is not self-confidence. This is the confidence from being firmly grounded in God. Our confidence is in Him.

come together

Open your group with prayer. This should be a brief, simple prayer in which you invite God to be with you as you meet.

As we have said in previous lessons, sharing our personal stories builds deeper connections among group members. Your story may be exactly what another person needs to hear to encourage or strengthen them. And listening to others' stories is an act of love and kindness to them—and could very well help them to grow spiritually. Begin your time together by using the following questions and activities to get people talking.

- What has surprised you most about this group? Where did God meet you over the last six weeks?

- Tell the group about a time you had to act, but were totally unprepared.

watch video session 6

beknownbiblestudy.com/videos

group discussion

grow together

Have someone in the group Read John 2:1-12.

- What did Jesus' mother know about her son?

- If you were the servant drawing out the water and giving it to the master of the feast, what might be running through your mind?

- Jesus' mother gave this instruction: "Whatever He says to you, do it." What is Jesus saying to you?

be together

- How has God changed your story during this six-week study? What new things is He asking you to do? What truth has transformed your heart? Think about specific steps you want to take to live a new story, to walk more closely with God so you can be part of His story and engaged in His kingdom.

- How has God put you in a situation where He says, "You're on. You've been made for this moment"?

- What is holding you back from doing what God has prepared you for?

- As we complete this study, what is your next step in pursuing God's direction for your life?

Since your next meeting will close out your time together in this study, take a few minutes to talk about your time of celebration and testimony sharing. Pass around a sign up sheet and encourage everyone to bring a dish to the celebration. It can be a brunch dish or heavy appetizer dish, depending on when you're group meets. Have the women prepare a short testimony this week of how they've seen the Lord work in their life during the six week study.

Close your meeting with prayer.

Close by praying for your prayer requests and take a couple of minutes to review the praises you have recorded over the past five weeks from your prayer journal. Spend some time thanking God for all He's done in your group during this study.

WEEK 6

daily study

DAY ONE

For the last four years, I've walked alongside a group of beautiful women as we studied God's Word every Monday morning. I love beginning my week worshiping God at church on Sunday and linking arms with these women Monday mornings. We've seen each other through celebrations, held each other as we've cried, interceded for babies and healings and walked with each other through seasons of the unknown. One thing that we've always prioritized is sharing prayer requests and praying for one another. I wish I could pull out my prayer journal and show you how many celebration dates I've put next to answered prayers over the years. We've seen God heal cancer, marriages, wombs of women who were told they would never conceive even with fertility treatments, and countless other requests for our children, our businesses, our ministries as wives, moms, and in our community of influence. We've never left our time together without sharing what we're praising Jesus for and what we're bringing to His feet.

A few times over the years we've committed to praying for each other at the same time every night regardless of where we are or what we're doing. One particular week we did this, we committed to getting on our knees, no matter where we were at 9 pm each night and pray for one another. To ask Jesus to meet the needs of our sisters by name. That week was a busy one for our family and I remember excusing myself at a restaurant during a double date and going to the bathroom to find a stall and pray. Another night we were at a high school football game and my 8:55pm reminder alarm went off. I left the stands in the middle of an intense game to go in search of a dark corner where I could kneel and pray. I remembered thinking how much easier it would be to be home every night to pray. But every time I came before the Lord on my knees that week, He would remind me of all the times in the Bible that Jesus retreated from the crowds to pray to His Father. He was not concerned with what people would think, He was only focused on the business of His Father.

WEEK 6 | SACRED LOVE

JESUS WAS ABOUT HIS FATHER'S BUSINESS

Let's begin today writing out this powerful scripture together. Words spoken by Jesus that speak to His commitment to the will of His Father. It also establishes the importance Jesus knowing who He was in His Father's eyes so He could fulfill His ministry here on earth.

Write John 6:38-40 in the margin.

Sweet friend, it's hard to believe we're already diving into week six together. What a journey the Lord has brought us on. I'm so thankful for your commitment to diving into His Word and allowing Him to minister to your heart. My prayer is that as we wrap up this week, Jesus brings us to a new level of closeness with Him. That something has shifted in your life, your love for Him has grown and your desire to chase after Him every morning becomes a time you long for as you go to sleep every night. I never saw myself as a morning person, but I would not trade my early morning hours in the presence of my Father for more minutes of sleep. I have experienced first-hand what giving the Lord the first fruits of my day has done in my life and I hope you are seeing it in yours too. God is so good, isn't He?!

As I've been studying for this week, I have the song, "You are Worthy of it All," playing on repeat. It has become like a prayer, "all of the glory, all of the glory, is yours, is yours, is yours. You are worthy of it all, you are worthy of it all, far from you are all things, and to you are all things, you deserve the glory." When we understand the worthiness of God, we never hesitate to seek Him and pray in all circumstances. Just as we phone a friend to talk through what's going on in our lives, Jesus desires that same connection with us.

Write 1 Thessalonians 5:16-18.

The Bible doesn't just talk about the importance of drawing near to God, Jesus modeled it during His time on earth. The first time we see this is in Luke 2 when He travels with His parents to Jerusalem for the Feast of the Passover. Jesus is twelve years old.

Let's read Luke 2:41-52 together.

How long had Jesus' family been traveling when they realized he was not with them? _____

Where do they find Him in Jerusalem? What is He doing?

How does Jesus respond to His parents when they find Him?

Write Luke 2:52.

At twelve years old Jesus already knew the importance of being in His Father's house. There's nothing insignificant about the timing of Him being there. The Passover was a celebration of God saving the Israelites from death through the sacrifice of a lamb and the mark of its scarlet blood on the doorpost of their home. Jesus knew there would come a time when He would take the place of that sacrificial lamb and die in atonement for our sins once and for all. The next time we see Jesus is in Luke 3:21. He's now thirty years old and eighteen years have passed since that moment in the temple courts. Although I can't help but wonder how many years after that one they found Jesus in the temple courts during the celebration of Passover. John the Baptist, Jesus' cousin, is baptizing people and preparing the way for Jesus.

WEEK 6 | SACRED LOVE

Write Luke 3:16 (NIV):

"John answered them all, "I baptize you with water. But _____ who is more _____ than I will come, the straps of whose sandals I am not worthy to untie. He will baptize you with the _____ _____ and _____.""

What is Jesus doing when John baptized Him (vs. 23)? _____

Yes! He is praying! Suddenly the sky opened up and the Holy Spirit descended on Him like a dove. I know we studied this in an earlier week, but I love how Matthew 3:16 says, "the Spirit of God descending like a dove and lighting on Him."

Jesus Prays. The Holy Spirit descends on Him. The Heavens open up and a voice from Heaven speaks, "This is my Son, whom I love; with Him I am well pleased."

Jesus knew exactly who He was! He knew who His father was. He also understood that through prayer He had direct access to His father in Heaven, the power of the Holy Spirit and He could always be reminded of whose He was. When we draw near to God, we will not only know who we are and whose we are, but we will receive the power of the Holy Spirit to walk in our calling. God didn't promise an easy ministry for Jesus during His time on earth, but He did promise to walk with Him. Jesus knew it was essential to chase after His Father in the secret place as a reminder of who He was and the strength He would need to fulfil His calling during His three years of active ministry on earth.

In Jesus' three years of active ministry, there are almost thirty scriptures that point to Him retreating to pray.

Write Luke 5:16.

When we draw near to God, we will not only know who we are and whose we are, but we will relieve the power of the Holy Spirit to walk in our calling.

If we want our identity to be in Jesus and we want to build the kingdom as He did, it begins with prayer. Let's look at a couple more verses together...

> **Matthew 14:23** - "After He had sent the crowds away, He went up on the mountain by Himself to _____; and when it was evening, He was there alone."

> **Mark 6:46** - After bidding them farewell, He left for the mountain to _____."

> **Luke 6:12** - "It was at this time that He went off to the mountain to _____, and He spent the whole night in _____ to God."

> **Mark 1:35** - "In the early morning, while it was still dark, Jesus got up, left the house, and went away to a secluded place, and was _____ there."

What does your prayer life look like?

When was a time you prayed for someone, and they saw healing, breakthrough, or victory?

I want to land the last moments of our time together today in Luke 23, looking at Jesus's final moments of His ministry. He had spent the whole night praying over and over asking His Father if there was any way to not have to endure the death He knew was coming. He pleaded with His Father so earnestly that the emotional anguish that He experienced caused drops of blood to pour out from his sweat. It's hard to even write this without tears, understanding Jesus' intense love for us and yet desperation in this moment, while also saying, "yet not my will, but yours be done."

The next morning Jesus is arrested, taken, and put on trial. Beaten, stripped, humiliated, crowned with thorns, and forced to carry His own cross up the mountain to His death. As He hung on the cross, the first thing we see Jesus do is to pray. "Father, forgive them, for they do not know what they are doing." (Luke 23:34). Gosh, I struggle with praying for people who have wronged me, and no one has nailed me to a cross. When we look up on the cross, we see Jesus praying and pleading with His Father on behalf of the people responsible for His death. They do not know you like I do, Father. Forgive their ignorance. One final time before Jesus takes His last breath, He prays one more time, committing His Spirit into the hands of His Father.

Diving Deeper

How are you committing your spirit into the hands of your Heavenly Father? How do you set aside time in your day to withdraw from the noise of the world and spend time in the Word and in prayer?

_____

_____

_____

_____

How often are we able to pray for others and on their behalf because we know who we are in Jesus? Our identity is firmly placed in Him, and we have a deep seeded desire for the women around us to experience Him the same way. I want to challenge you to set aside a time every day that you're going to retreat and pray. Even if it's just for five minutes and pray for three people the Lord puts on your heart. Set an reminder and commit to praying for them every day. Watch what God does!

Posture of Prayer

In your prayer time today, ask the Lord to put three people on your heart. He wants you to be praying for this week. Then spend some time in His presence thanking Him for going to the cross on your behalf.

DAY TWO

(BE) KNOWN

I always knew I wanted to be a mother. From the time I was little, I used to say that when I grew up, I wanted to be a teacher and a mother. No one prepares you for the first time you hold your first baby in your arms. Holding our sweet Katelyn was nothing like seeing her profile image on the ultrasound screen moving around inside my belly. Yes, I carried her, but then I gave birth to her and suddenly I was carrying her in a new way. Throughout the years of her life, how I've carried her has looked different, but my intentionality to do so has never wavered. Every day I make it my mission to cover her and her room in prayer, carve out time to sit and listen to her day and look for ways I can meet her spoken and unspoken needs. The Lord has also so graciously opened the door for opportunities to minister and teach her. What I have learned as a mother though is that the greatest way I can teach her is to model what it looks like to emulate Jesus to her.

For so many years I didn't think I could be both a teacher and a mother. I saw them as two separate jobs, one inside the household and the other outside it. That feeling that I could only choose one gifting, one calling, one passion at a time. It crippled me for so long. Even when I was running a business that empowered women *to have more work/life balance and freed up their time to work and still have space to be a mom, I felt mom guilt that somehow I wasn't doing something I should've been for my children. Here's the beautiful thing that the Lord showed me; I didn't have to choose. I could use my gifts both inside and outside my home to honor God in the gifts He's given me and the calling He's stirred up in me. The more I prioritized being a kingdom changer in my home, the more opportunities God opened doors for outside of my home. He wants to do the same for you!*

JESUS NEVER WAVERS

Yesterday we studied scripture that showed us how Jesus never wavered on His identity. He knew He was His father's son, who came to earth for a purpose and, once fulfilled He would return to heaven to be with His father. If we had to sum it up in one sentence it would be: Jesus came to earth so that we would have the opportunity to know Him, experience Him, and be transformed by Him. From the time He was in Mary's womb to when He ascended into heaven after His resurrection, He never wavered from that purpose. He came for our salvation. Period, full stop. As a result of His ministry, people encountered Him during His time on earth and when He was gone they would continue to tell others about their need for Him too.

What is your favorite story in the Bible of an interaction Jesus had with someone that left them transformed?

How do you view the crucifixion? Do you ever think about the magnitude of what that day was like for Jesus?

I love that Jesus never asks us to walk a road He's never traveled before us. He doesn't ask us to model a behavior He never did when He was here on earth. I'm not talking about the flipping the table moments, I'm talking about the way that He never changed course during His three years of ministry.

Jesus could've easily changed His mind as the time rapidly approached His betrayal. After all, He is God. Yet, His grace and His love for us, outweighed the weight of the cross: physically, emotionally, mentally, and spiritually.

In week three we talked about how each of us was created by God on purpose for a purpose and that your creator, who so intricately created you, always had a beautiful plan for your life. Today we're going to look at how Jesus walked in His purpose before and after His resurrection and ascension into Heaven.

JESUS WAS CONFIDENT IN HIS CALLING

During His three years of ministry, Jesus never questioned His Father. There's never an accusation or a time when Jesus says we don't deserve for Him to go to the cross on our behalf. Jesus pushed back against religious views, Pharisees, and those who saw and didn't believe, but He never pushed back against His Father or His purpose here on earth.

Write Jeremiah 17:7.

Jesus never doubted himself or changed Himself to please other people. Does that mean we can walk around behaving however we want and expect Jesus to bless our ministry? No, it does not! Jesus spoke the truth in grace and love, always with the intention of drawing people to Him and transforming their lives.

Write Hebrews 10:35-36

Jesus came to redeem the lost. He came for the salvation of the sinners. This is the heart of how Jesus wants us to live as well. He wants us to chase after the lost and love them into Heaven.

WEEK 6 | SACRED LOVE

Write Luke 19:10

Philippians 1:6 - "being _____ of this, that he who began a good work in you will carry it on to completion until the day of Christ Jesus."

JESUS WALKED IN HUMILITY

Jesus repeatedly tells people not to spread the word about Him after He performed miracles. He knew it wasn't about the miracle, it was about their salvation. Jesus didn't want people walking around focused on His acts of healing, but on how He could completely change and transform their whole life. Jesus always points back to being about His Father's business.

Write Mark 1:44

Jesus was always serving others. He insisted that we need to have a heart to serve others first, to be great in His kingdom. He is looking for those who are faithful with little because Jesus knows that if we can be faithful with a little, we will be faithful with much. A servant's heart is not one that needs recognition or accolades for giving of your time, talent, or treasure to further God's kingdom.

Write Mark 10:45

Jesus suffered and was rejected. He doesn't promise a smooth, easy-going life if we're going to serve His kingdom. He does promise the reward in Heaven is worth the suffering we endure while on earth.

Write John 16:33.

JESUS WALKED BOLDLY IN HIS CALLING

Jesus traveled far distances, oftentimes going out of the way, to meet people where they were at. He wasn't dictated by time, but by people's salvation.

Write John 4:3-4

Remember when we talked about the woman at the well? Jesus didn't have to go through Samaria on His way to Galilee from Judea, but He did and that beautiful woman's life was changed forever. She went out and told an entire village to come and hear Jesus speak and they also believed.

He willingly went to the cross even though He was innocent. He endured so much pain and suffering on our behalf and we're so quick to complain when people don't zipper in the school carpool line or when we don't like the message the Pastor preaches on a Sunday morning.

Write John 18:11

WEEK 6 | SACRED LOVE

Jesus had the beautiful audacity to tell the criminal hanging next to him that his belief would find him in heaven with Jesus when he died. He came for our salvation until His last breath.

Write Luke 23:42-43

There are some of you who have been going through this study and you can feel the stirring on your hearts. The Lord is moving in and through you in a new way. You have spent time and energy trying to make things happen for yourself – your marriage, family, and your job. You're feeling the overwhelming weight of it all. Sweet friend, the Lord wants to release all that from you. He wants you to choose to chase after Him in the secret place, so you can be truly known by Him. If that's you. Your heart is speeding up and you can hear His still small voice calling you to let go, let Him in, give Him control I want to invite you to re-dedicate your life to Jesus. Let's take a moment and pray this prayer together.

> *Jesus, I love you so much. Thank you for convicting my spirit. I have been trying for far too long to do this on my own. To control the outcomes of my marriage, my family, my job, my friendships, and how you want me to serve in the church. I'm ready to surrender it all to you. Jesus, I ask that you'll take over as Lord in my life. I want to be known by you. To hear your voice. So, I can find my passion in who you say I am and how you want to use my life for the glory of your kingdom. I rededicate my life to you today. Thank you for your forgiveness. Fill me with your Holy Spirit. – Amen*

Some of you were gifted this study or invited to join friends as they go through it and you don't know that you believe in God. You've been struggling with thoughts of if He truly is real and if He really does love you. But as you've studied His Word the last six weeks you can feel Him tugging on your heart, inviting you into the more that He has for you. His deep love for you, that took Him to the cross to die for you, has you longing to know more about

Him. Jesus wants you to know that invitation is right here, in front of you. He's ready when you are. Friend, that day is today! I want to invite you to make the best decision you'll ever make in your life. One that will fill you with peace, joy, and hope in complete and unexplainable ways. If that's you and you're ready to dedicate your life to Jesus, I want to invite you to pray this prayer with me.

Jesus, I thank you. For loving me, even when I've struggled to love myself. For chasing after me, even when you were the last person on my mind. Thank you for opening up my heart to you. For showing me how much you love me. That you died on a cross for me. For my sins. So I can be set free and live a life forgiven. Thank you that you chose me for your kingdom. I invite you into my heart today. I ask that you would fill me, guide me, and use me for your kingdom. I want to be known by you. I pray that the people around me would see the change in me and I will be able to tell them about you, Jesus. Fill me with your Holy Spirit. I want to be your daughter, heir to your kingdom. I love you! – Amen!

If you prayed either prayer today. Congratulations, sweet sister! Welcome to the kingdom! I am so proud of you. There are so many women who have been praying for you and for this moment and we're all celebrating with you. If you made this decision today, I want to encourage you to tell someone. If you're not plugged into a church, begin looking for a church to join. If you're in Southern California, I want to invite you to join me at Ocean's Church. We meet every Sunday at 9 am and 11 am. If you don't know where to begin looking for a church, please reach out to me online. My team and I would love to help you find a church home!

Diving Deeper

Why are you thankful for your salvation? Where in your calling do you need to live more like Jesus? Do you need more confidence, humility, and boldness? Why?

_____
_____
_____
_____
_____
_____
_____

Jesus came and died so that you and I would know Him. Not only know Him by name but also know His presence. That we would be transformed by the power of His blood, shed on the cross for our sins. He knew that if we were truly transformed by Him, our greatest desire would be to see others receive that same gift. It would drive the very core of our being and everything we do in our businesses, homes, communities, and friendships would point people to Jesus.

Posture of Prayer

Put on some worship music as you journal today. Spend some time in Jesus' presence today asking Him to show you areas in your life you need to walk more confidently, humbly, and boldly in the calling on your life. Thank Him for your salvation and for dying on the cross for your redemption. Continue praying for the three women He put on your heart yesterday to be praying for.

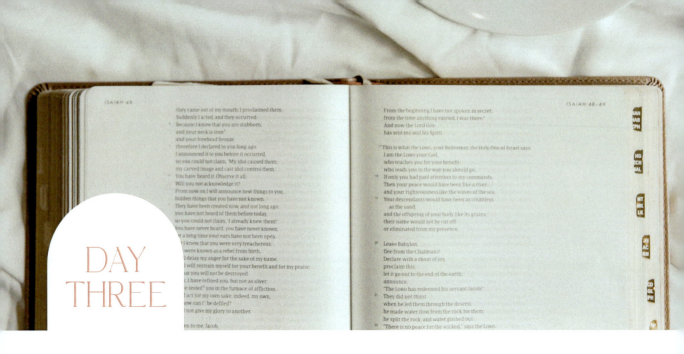

DAY THREE

For most of my life, I've had the honor of being a part of different women's and couples' Bible studies. I love studying the Word with other believers. There's something about hearing the faith journeys of others and praying with them that elevates my faith and draws me closer to the Lord. I've also had the opportunity to study God's Word by going through Bible studies that some incredible women of faith have written: Beth Moore. Priscilla Schrier, Angie Smith, Jackie Perry Hill, and there are so many more. I've always been content to show up, let others lead, and go about my day. Then in the spring of 2022 a woman in the faith I greatly admire, Beth Redman, asked me if I would be part of the leadership team for an eight-week study on 1 and 2 Corinthians. I knew from the first night we met, laid the foundation for the weeks ahead, and spent time in prayer that God was about to do something beautiful. Not just in the life of these women, but in my own as well.

Over the next several weeks I had the privilege of seeing God move in mighty ways. As a co-leader, I got to serve the women, wash dishes, pray over them, love on them and be a part of letting them just come and soak in the presence of Jesus. They could arrive, be served, and do nothing but enjoy a night out of their home where they didn't need to cook, clean, or *put their littles to bed. We had the privilege of doing it all for them and gosh the conversations around the table, listening to people contend for their families, marriages, children, and callings on their lives were so beautiful to hear. Towards the end of the study, we began commissioning the women one by one, praying over them, and washing their feet. It truly felt like a season of being the hands and feet of Jesus. As I poured out week after week, God began to pour into me every morning as I met Him faithfully at my dining room table at 5:30 am each morning. I picked up my pen and began writing again, only this time the Lord asked me to turn my book into a six-week Bible study first, and then we would go back and finish my book. I'm in such awe of His goodness and His kindness. This study is an outpouring of a drenching in the glory of the Holy Spirit*

JESUS WAS UNIQUELY GIFTED

Jesus knew His gifts and He used them everywhere else He went.

In week four we talked about our unique gifts, both natural and supernatural. They come directly from our creator and are woven into us from the time we were created in our mother's womb. While we might not see the manifestation of our supernatural gifts until we get older or begin asking for the Lord to bring them out of us, they still exist in us and we have access to all of them through the power of the Holy Spirit. Acts 2 wasn't just for the benefit of the early church. It was just the beginning of a power we all have access to until such time Jesus comes back for us, and we get to live in His glory forever and ever, Amen!

We are able to walk in those gifts because Jesus showed us what it looked like during His ministry. Today we're going to look at some of the ways Jesus used His gifts, both natural and supernatural to serve others.

Write Galatians 5:22-23

Looking at all the stories in the Bible we've read together and others you are familiar with, when is an example of Jesus walking in the fruit of the Spirit?

Jesus would never encourage us to live a life of love, joy, peace, patience, kindness, goodness, faithfulness, gentleness, and self-control if His life didn't reflect them. He went out of His way often: across the Sea of Galilee, through Samaria, stopping under trees, having dinner with the lost, turning water into wine, casting out demons, healing the sick, blind, and demon-possessed. Who do we go out of the way to serve while claiming a deep love for Jesus?

What are some ways God is calling you to serve others without expecting any credit for doing so?

Write Matthew 5:15-16

> We should desire to live a life that allows His fruit to bloom on our vine..

We're called, not to hide the light of Jesus, but to shine it wherever we go so that all who see it and experience it will see what you have done but give glory to God in Heaven. We should desire to live a life that allows His fruit to bloom on our vine ultimately drawing others to Jesus. I will not claim that this is an easy task, the fruit isn't always visible on my vine, but what God looks at is the posture of our heart. Is it the desire of our heart to serve the kingdom of heaven by serving others that His fruit would be visible in our lives? The more we spend time in our Father's presence, living a life that produces this kind of fruit will begin to flow more naturally out of us, without us even realizing it.

Turn in your Bibles with me to Matthew 14:13-21.

I love that we began our time together in Matthew 14 with the invitation to come. To step boldly into what God has for you. That first comes from knowing who He says you are. Now as our time together comes to a close, we find ourselves back in Matthew 14, only today we're going to look at a story in the Bible that

WEEK 6 | SACRED LOVE

shows Jesus' desire to serve others. That they would know Him, be transformed by Him, and His glory would be seen on them as they go out and tell others about Him.

Why was Jesus trying to retreat by boat to a private place in verse 13? (Look back to vs 10-12) _____

What happens when Jesus gets to shore? _____

How does Jesus respond?

> ## Matthew 14:14 (NIV)
>
> "When Jesus landed and saw a large crowd, he had _____ on them and _____ their sick."

Jesus has just found out that His cousin John has been beheaded and He retreats to have some time alone to grieve. Large crowds find out where He's going and instead of arriving to peace and quiet, He is met with people looking for healing and to hear Him speak. It would've been so easy in that moment for Jesus to become angry and rebuke the people. Or have the disciples send them all away so He could grieve, but instead verse 14 says He showed compassion on them. His immediate concern was for the suffering of those right in front of Him and He began healing the sick. Evening approaches and the disciples are encouraging Jesus to send the crowd away so they can get Him to a place where He can rest for the night.

How does Jesus respond? (vs. 16) _____

Jesus is trying to teach the disciples that part of using your gifts to bring people into the Kingdom is that it's much more important to have a heart that is disposed to serving others. Not just showing up, leading a couple of worship songs, preaching the gospel, praying, and sending people on their way. What are you doing to nourish their bodies and their souls? Jesus often gathered people around a table for a meal. He dined with sinners like Zacchaeus and those who loved Him, like Mary, Martha, Lazarus, and the disciples. His mission at the table never changed. Jesus emphasized that He was the bread of life and those who chased after Him would always be sustained. He is also the living water. The Holy Spirit is never stagnant, nor is the Word of God. They're alive and breathing and flow in and through us so we can invite people to join us at our table, nourish their bodies as we nourish their souls in hopes that they walk away having encountered just a little bit of the Jesus that lives in us.

That day, despite His grief having lost His cousin John, Jesus healed the sick, He spoke about His Father and the Kingdom of Heaven, and He served them all a meal. I love how verse twenty says that they all ate until they were filled and there was still food remaining! Jesus never gives us just enough; He always provides more than we could ever ask for.

Why do you think it's significant that Matthew points out that everyone ate until they were full and there were still leftovers?

How can we connect what Jesus did that day for the crowd of 5,000 with how we are to respond to others as we walk in our natural and supernatural gifts?

What did you learn from seeing Jesus' example of how you are to walk in the gifts He's given you while here on earth?

Jesus modeled this for us all the way to the cross. He shares a final meal with the disciples to nourish their souls one last time, promising that when He goes, something greater, the Holy Spirit, will come in His place. Then He washes their feet! An individual blessing for each man who had walked with Him for three years, traveling and doing ministry with Him so faithfully. They came, never knowing what that walking with Jesus would look like but ended up with their lives forever marked by Him. They had become His best friends and His brothers. That last night together Jesus washed their feet knowing that one man would betray Him and turn Him into the authorities, one would deny Him three times and several of them would scatter and leave Him as He was sentenced to die.

In the garden, He heals the ear of the servant of the high priest that Peter cuts off defending Jesus when they came to arrest Him. A priest who claimed to be a religious man, coming to arrest Jesus experienced a miracle. I wonder how that impacted the rest of that man's life, especially after watching Jesus die and then knowing He rose again three days later just as He said He would. If Jesus, knowing He came as the ultimate sacrifice for our sins, never swayed from using His gifts to serve others, how much more must we also strive to do the same?

Diving Deeper

How do you want to model Jesus as you use your gifts? Where do you struggle to model Jesus in your life? How do you need to change the posture in which you approach using your gifts to serve others?

_____

_____

_____

_____

When Jesus appears to His disciples after His resurrection He says to them, "Peace be with you! As the Father has sent me, I am sending you. And with that he breathed on them and said, "Receive the Holy Spirit." Perhaps you're in a season of waiting to see how God is going to use your gifts to fulfill His calling on your life or maybe you're already fully living in the calling. The question is how are you using those gifts in the waiting or in the doing to nourish all those around you? Jesus used His gifts to elevate others and we are called to do the same. I want to challenge you today to look at areas of your life where you have used your gifts to serve for personal gain so the glory can point back to you rather than your Heavenly Father.

Posture of Prayer

Spend some time praying today and asking the Lord how He wants you to be using your gifts to serve His kingdom. Repent for times you've served only for personal glory and ask the Lord to give you a heart for using your gifts to serve so others will see evidence of Him in your life. Thank Him for dying on the cross for you, so that you could have a deeper connection with Him.

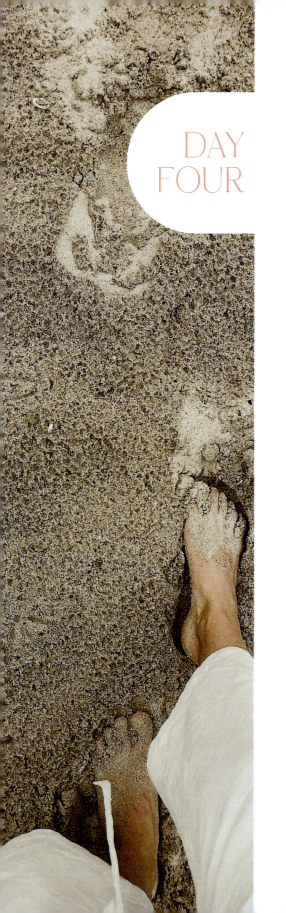

DAY FOUR

(BE)KNOWN

There have been so many moments in the last three years where I've questioned what God was doing. Even though I love my life and my family whole heartedly, if I'm being honest there have been many moments where my spirit has felt as though there was something more I had yet to discover. There have been so many desperate prayers prayed in my prayer closet for the Lord to give me confirmation that He had not forgotten all the dreams and visions He had put on my heart. As the months went by during the first two years, I felt the weight of my obedience to surrender things in my life; my business, friendships, my future, and my book. The very same book He put on my heart and asked me to write! I kept serving and seeking Him. When I was asked to co-lead a small group of women at our church, I prayed and said yes. When Erin and I were asked if we would write the curriculum, we prayed and said yes. The first curriculum led to a second small group curriculum and our little group of women on Friday mornings doubled in size. I found myself spending most days praying and thanking Jesus for entrusting us with the hearts of these women who had a deep thirst for the Holy Spirit.

Right before my birthday in March of 2022, my husband and I completely overhauled our lives by looking at our nutrition and we began working with a health coach. Two weeks later we were at lunch celebrating my birthday when a conversation led to what it would look like to write and self-publish a women's Bible study before the book. I had been stuck mid-way through writing my book for almost six months so the idea of switching gears seemed equally exciting and terrifying. I told the people *around the table if the Lord began waking me up at 5:30 am, I would begin writing. Two weeks later the Lord began waking me up at, you guessed it, 5:30 am and I began to write. As I sit here ten weeks later, writing the final two days of our study and down over twenty pounds, I can see the fruit of how the Lord used this season to completely transform my mind, body, soul, and spirit. The more I sought healing and forgiveness, began working out every day, and cleared my body of foods that weren't serving me, the more He filled those places with Him.*

IN EVERY SEASON THERE IS MORE

Sweet friend, how I have prayed for you over the last couple of months as I've been writing. There have also been an incredible group of women who have interceded in prayer on your behalf that as you faithfully studied His Word, Jesus would meet you in a deeper way than ever before. From this study, you would feel shifts in your heart, your home, your relationships, and your prayer life. The Lord told me that so many of you would start this study with cracks in your foundation, but He would fill in those cracks and make you whole. You won't leave the way you came. Hallelujah! His greatest desire is for you to know Him and hear His voice.

This week we've talked about how Jesus knew His Father and He came to fulfill a purpose, using the gifts (natural and supernatural) His Father had given Him. Jesus' season of ministry might have been short, but it greatly impacted so many. I sometimes wonder if Jesus ever had conversations with His father about the urgency to get started so they could reach more people. After all, He was almost thirty years old before we saw Him baptized by His cousin John, begin calling His disciples and perform His first miracle. Did He ever have conversations with His Father about beginning sooner or was he hesitant to begin because He knew His time in ministry would be short?

When was a season of your life where you knew the Lord was calling you into something new, but you didn't know when you were going to walk in that calling?

How did you chase after Jesus during that season? If you didn't, why was that?

Let's look at John 2:1-11 together.

> "Woman, why do you involve me?" Jesus replied. "My hour has not yet come."
>
> *John 2:4*

Jesus and His disciples accompany His mother Mary to a wedding in Cana. It was customary in those days for a wedding celebration to last up to a week with no shortage of food and wine. On the third day of the celebration Mary, seeing that they've run out of wine, goes to Jesus to tell Him.

How does Jesus respond to His mother? (vs. 4) _____

Jesus responds to His mother saying that His hour had not yet come. Time, as it's used in this passage, is translated to the Greek word hora (ho'-rah), which means, "a certain definite time or season." Remember supernatural time is not like time here on earth. When Jesus comes to earth He walks into a different time zone, one that is finite rather than infinite. He knows that when His "season" or time begins, so does the path to His crucifixion. Mary knows her son has come to save the lost and knowing this she tells the servants to do whatever Jesus tells them to do. Jesus responds by having them fill the six ceremonial jugs with water and giving it to the Master of the Banquet to taste. Ceremonial jugs were traditionally used for the washing and cleansing of the guest's hands.

When poured out what does the water turn to? _____

Jesus' first miracle is turning water into wine. He has the servants fill the six ceremonial jugs that hold 20-30 gallons of water and are normally used to cleanse the hands of the guests with water and as it's poured out it turns into wine. This is significant because we know that Jesus came as living water and would one day hang on the cross and shed His blood (wine) for our sins. When we come to Jesus in repentance, He washes us with His water and blood to cleanse us and purify us, bringing us closer to righteousness.

What can we learn from Jesus about how we should lean into the presence of the Holy Spirit in each season?

1. We don't always know the timing, but we need to be ready.

Jesus points out to His mother that His time had not yet come, but He still performed the miracle. From this miracle, He revealed His glory and His disciples believed. In that moment, these young men who dropped their nets to follow Jesus fully understood the magnitude of that commitment. They went from deciding to travel with a friend to understanding that there would never be anything normal about following Jesus. They had just experienced the extraordinary.

Write 1 Peter 3:15 below.

If someone were to ask you if you're ready to share the gospel with someone if they asked, how would you respond? Why?

2. Obey without questioning.

Jesus never questions His father's timing or His calling. We talked about this earlier this week. In this moment we see Jesus say his time has not yet come, but He knows what He came to earth to do, and He performs the miracle knowing that. He's not obeying His mother by performing this miracle, although He does honor her while speaking with her. He's obeying His Father in heaven. This moment happens and it triggers the beginning of His ministry. When we walk in obedience to God, the timing or the action we're taking doesn't always make sense in the moment but rest assured God has a bigger purpose and plan for it.

Write Deuteronomy 28:1 below.

How are you living a life of full obedience to the Lord?

3. Jesus has something more.

Jesus didn't just turn the water into ordinary wine. When the servants took the cup to the master of the banquet, he said it's customary to bring out the cheaper wine as the days go on, but the bridegroom had saved the best for last. In the same way, Jesus did this for the Bridegroom, He does the same for us. Everything He does is for the good of those who love Him.

Write Ephesians 3:20 below.

In what ways are you struggling to believe that God has more for you in this season?

4. Everything should point to God's Glory

Jesus didn't turn the water into wine so that He would get the praise. If He had, He could've brought the jars before the wedding guests, asked the servants to fill them, and then poured the wine himself. Instead, He instructs the servants to do the filling and take a cup to the master of the banquet. At that moment He revealed His glory to those who were ready to believe. Like Jesus, we should be doing the work to build the kingdom, not for our glory or accolades but to point people to Jesus, so they can encounter Him as you have.

Write John 2:11 below.

Diving Deeper

In what ways do you need Jesus' strength to stay faithful and obedient to the calling He has stirred within you? How does knowing Jesus only spent three years of His life in active ministry change your perspective in your waiting? How are you equipping yourself for the calling in this season?

_____
_____
_____
_____

John 10:10 in The Passion Translation says, "A thief has only one thing in mind - he wants to steal, slaughter, and destroy. But I have come to give you everything in abundance, more than you expect - life in its fullness until you overflow!" Isn't that just the most beautiful picture of how good God is?! It speaks to His intentionality in all things. He turned the water into the best wine. He came and died so that we might experience His love and redemption in our lives. He works all things together for the good of those who love Him. God's goodness isn't just to fill you to the brim, it's to bring overflow and abundance!

Posture of Prayer

Grab your journal and a cozy blanket and spend some time asking the Lord for His timing for the plans He has for your life. Ask Him to help you lead a life in the seasons of waiting and doing that honors others and glorifies Him. Then spend some time thanking Him for everything He's doing in your life to prepare you for what He has next.

> "A thief has only one thing in mind - he wants to steal, slaughter, and destroy. But I have come to give you everything in abundance, more than you expect - life in its fullness until you overflow!"
> *John 10:10*

(BE)KNOWN

DAY FIVE

As we prepare for our time together to come to a close...

It's so important when we do the work to deepen our relationship with our Heavenly Father that we both seal and celebrate what God has done. We're going to do that by taking communion together and sharing a testimony of how the Lord has moved in your life through this study. Friend, this is a beautiful and necessary step of gratitude to our Heavenly Father. If you've walked through this study individually, I encourage you to take communion, write out your testimony and share it with someone. I invite you to email me and share it with me, I would love nothing more than to celebrate with you!

If you've been going through this study with a group of women, I recommend waiting to do day five together. Celebrate with a meal, or even sweet treats, worship together, share your testimonies, and leave space for a time of communion. It's powerful when we vocalize the breakthrough we're having and the ways the Lord is moving in our lives! And it's so important that, as women, we link arms and celebrate those victories with each other.

If you have women in your group who need to rededicate their lives to Jesus or perhaps, they don't know the Lord, there is a guide you can use on pages 215-216 to help prepare the hearts of the women for communion. Partaking of the Lord's Supper first requires us to examine our hearts, but also offers an opportunity to make sure that each woman has a personal relationship with Jesus. Take time to worship, pray and prepare the space to invite the Holy Spirit in before sharing The Lord's Supper.

I wish I was going to be there with each one of you! I have no doubt your time of celebration is going to be so beautiful and so powerful. I'm so proud of you all for putting in the work to dive deeper into your relationship with Jesus these last six weeks.

Today is bittersweet for me. I have been committed to praying regularly for any woman who may pick up this study and that includes you, for the last two years. Praying that the Lord has met you in new and unexpected ways. That these six weeks have deepened your faith and given you a deep hunger to open His Word daily and soak up the time in His presence. The prayer of my heart has always been that as we've read and declared scripture together it's given you a new excitement and confidence to go dig into His promises and continue to journal your prayers. There's nothing like seeing dated miracles next to God's promises for your life.

Sweet friends, this is an exciting day of celebration of who God says you are and His calling on your life!! He has great plans for your life and these past few weeks have only been the beginning. Do you believe that?! Today we're going to seal this time and all the work Jesus has done in your life by celebrating with a time of communion. If you have crackers or bread and juice (or wine), take a few minutes, and go collect them.

Jesus' love is so sacred and unwavering, and it was that love that carried Him to the cross. It sustained Him as He stood trial, was stripped, beaten, humiliated, mocked, and hung on the cross for you.

John 15:13 puts it so beautifully, it says, "No one has greater love [nor stronger commitment] than to lay his own life down for his friends." (AMP)

I just love the emphasis on not only a great love for you but also a strong commitment to you. Thank you, Heavenly Father! There is no greater man than Jesus. No greater love than that which He possesses for you. He is the same yesterday, today, and forever. Never wavering or changing. Jesus will never leave you or forsake you. He will always meet you wherever you're at. Will you choose to continue to love Him in the deserts and valleys as well as the mountain top moments?

In those final days, Jesus gathered for a meal with His disciples one last time before Judas betrayed Him. During their meal together He not only nourished their bodies and their souls, but He served them one last time washing their feet.

Write John 13:1 in the margin.

> Having loved His own who were in the world, He now showed them the full extent of His love.

Having loved His own who were in the world, He now showed them the full extent of His love. Can you feel the weight of that impact? Just the thought of Jesus washing the feet of the disciples who had so diligently walked with Him for over three years has me doubling over with emotion. He washed even the feet of the men who would desert Him at the cross, the man who would deny Him (Peter), and the man who would betray Him (Judas). You are worthy of the same love. Oh, how He loves you so much, sweet friend. There's nothing in this world that can separate you from Him!

As we get ready to partake in communion, I want to invite you to turn on some worship music and take a few minutes to thank Jesus for everything He has done in your life in the last six weeks. If there's anything lingering that you need to let go of, I pray you'll surrender it once and for all. Let's choose to walk in freedom and victory!!!

Take some time to linger in God's presence before we take communion together.

If you have your elements near you, go ahead and grab them and let's take communion together. 1 Corinthians 11:23-26 says,

"I have handed down to you what came to me by direct revelation from the Lord himself. The same night in which he was handed over, he took bread and gave thanks. Then he distributed it to the disciples and said, "Take it and eat your fill. It is my body, which is given for you. Do this to remember me." He did the same with the cup of wine after supper and said, "This cup seals the new covenant with my blood. Drink it—and whenever you drink this, do it to remember me." Whenever you eat this bread and drink this cup, you are retelling the story, proclaiming our Lord's death until he comes."

When you're ready go ahead and eat the bread and drink from the cup.

As we close our precious time together, I want to read these words from Jesus in John 17 over you.

"My prayer is not for them alone. I pray also for those who will believe in me through their message, that all of them may be one, Father, just as you are in me, and I am in you. May they also be in us so that the world may believe that you have sent me. I have given them the glory that you gave me, that they may be one as we are one— I in them and you in me—so that they may be brought to complete unity. Then the world will know that you sent me and have loved them even as you have loved me." - John 17:20-23

Now it's your turn, friend. I want you to use the empty space below to write a testimony of what God has done in your life through this study. How have you seen Him grow you, stretch you, and change you? What doors has He opened and invited you to walk through?

_____
_____
_____
_____
_____
_____
_____
_____
_____
_____
_____

Sweet daughter of Jesus, heir to His Kingdom, may the Lord bless you and keep you; The Lord make His face shine upon you, And be abundantly gracious to you; The Lord, who loves you beyond measure life up His countenance upon you, And give you peace, joy, and confidence as you boldly walk in who He says you are, in full assurance of the calling upon your life and the gifts He will use to build His kingdom in every season of your life. Amen!

Go in Peace and Live Boldly for Him!

Thank you, Jesus! To you be the glory, forever and ever, Amen.

WEEK SEVEN

celebration of God's goodness

come together

Today is such an exciting day! Your group is going to gather, first around the table to break bread together and then to celebrate God's goodness over the last six weeks. This is a day of celebration, so I encourage you to make it special. Set the table, pick up festive paper plates, maybe even print a verse that encouraged your group during the study for each woman to take home. We want to remember what the Lord has done over the course of the study.

If your group still needs to make decisions about continuing to meet after this session, have that discussion now. Talk about what you will study, who will lead, and when you will begin meeting again.

Take some time to worship together. We have included a worship playlist in the appendix if you need guidance on a song to pick this week.

Open your group with prayer. This should be a brief, simple prayer, in which you invite God to be with you as you meet.

grow together

Remember this is a time of celebration. Have each woman take a few minutes to share a testimony of what the Lord has done in her life the last six weeks. Where has she been challenged to grow? How has her relationship with the Lord changed? Be sure to celebrate each woman after they share and leave space for a couple women in the group to affirm the growth they've seen. This serves as way to celebrate the boldness to be vulnerable. I know this is going to be such a special time with your group. God is so good!

If you would like to share your testimony with our team, we would love to hear from you. You can email us at hello@alissacircle.com

Take some time to pray together and for each other.

This is a beautiful way for the Lord to seal the work He's done in all of you through this study.

appendices

name chart

NAME	ORIGIN (Hebrew or Greek)	MEANING
Adam		
Eve		
Joshua		
Peter (Simon Peter)		
Matthew		
Andrew		
James, son of Zebedee		
John		
Saul		
Paul		
Deborah		
Mary		
Elizabeth		
Esther		
Ruth		
Jesus		

APPENDIX

leader guide

intro week | culture & connection

Set the culture; create comfort and community among the women, and set expectations for confidentiality and contribution. The focus on this day should be ice breaker questions, worship, prayer and giving a "lay of the land" of the curriculum you will all be studying together. I would recommend having coffee/tea and some goodies or snacks to make your first time together feel like the breaking of bread. If you feel led, share a short devotional from scripture you're studying in your personal quiet time with the group.

week 1 | the invitation to come

Jesus, our creator, is inviting us all to come to the secret place and discover what it means to be known by Him. Where the world would like to label us to keep us from stepping into our calling, Jesus reminds us that only He who created us gets to name us and He whispers our name in our ear and reminds us that we are His.

Day 1: He Gave You Your Name

1. What does your name mean? In what ways do you resonate with the meaning of your name?
2. What does "Being Known" mean to you?
3. Knowing that the God who created you also names you, how does that changehe way you look at the meaning of your name?

Use this to guide conversation and discussion through weekly homework.

Day 2: Prompting Leads to Preparation

1. When you think of the names you've given yourself or allowed others to give you, which ones are still stuck with you today?
2. What holds you back from believing God has a calling on your life?
3. In Joshua 1:3-5, five promises are listed, which one did you need to be reminded of?
4. What promises has the Lord been whispering in your ear?

Day 3: His Invitation is Intentional

1. Review Luke 5:1-10: How does knowing Jesus grew up with so many of the same experiences and expectations we did help you relate to Him better?
2. Focus Luke 5:4b; Invitation and obedience: Where do you feel Jesus has not provided for your needs?
3. Where is Jesus wanting to stretch you and prepare you for launch?

Day 4: Come and Experience

1. What doubts in your life have become a roadblock for you?
2. What do you think is going through Matthew's mind? If you were him, standing there with Peter, what would you be saying to Peter?
3. What fears have been holding you back from truly stepping into the deep with Jesus?

Day 5: God's Dreams for Us are Bigger

1. Have women share how they rewrote Jeremiah 33:3 in their margin? Discuss.
2. Do you need a walk on water moment with Jesus? What new things do you feel Him stirring in your heart, yet you're unable to step out on the water?
3. In what ways have you identified with Matthew in your life?
4. How do you see God's role in your life?

week 2 | Letting Him Name Us

Your creator, who named you, who calls you by name, desires for you to know Him as deeply as He knows you. The enemy is always at word to make us believe that we can't have full access to our Heavenly Father because of our past, but that could not be further from the truth.

Day 1: Hide and Seek

1. Read Romans 8:38-39 together. Discuss some of the areas/things in your life that you avoid talking to Jesus about.
2. Look at Psalm 139:1-7. Which of these verses is hard for you to digest that your creator could feel this way about you?
3. Talk about the women with the issue of bleeding. Focus on her desperate need for Jesus in that moment regardless of what it meant for those around her.
4. How do you feel convicted that you've been hiding from Jesus?

Day 2: Don't Give Your Identity to What Does Not Matter

5. What is an idol and what is worship? In what ways do we need to be careful not to allow the worship of worldly things to take the place of worshiping God?
6. Who does God say we are? Which word(s) are promises you're standing on?
7. Acts 9:1-9: recap Saul's encounter with God and His reformation.
8. Reclaiming your name. Have women read what they wrote.

Day 3: Declaring all Things New

1. Read 2 Corinthians 3:18. Have women share their Declarations
2. Talk about the Office of the Prophet vs the gift of Prophecy. How are we operating in that gift, in alignment with God's Word?
3. Is walking in this gifting difficult for you, why or why not?

Day 4: How do you Fill Your Love Tank?

1. Spiritual discipline is your love tank. What does your spiritual discipline in this season look like?
2. Deborah knew God in the secret place and it was there the Lord prepared her each day for her calling. What does your secret place look like? What components make it special?
3. Who you are in the secret place is what pours out of you when you're around others. What does the overflow of your secret place look like?

APPENDIX

4. What characteristics did you see in Deborah that are encouraging you to seek God in a deeper way in your own life?

Day 5: Sitting at His Feet

1. Read Luke 10:38-41 together. What must it have been like for Mary to experience physically sitting at Jesus' feet?

2. Discuss the differences between the way the two women approach Jesus. Why do you think Jesus allowed Martha to get to that tipping point?

3. When was a time you encountered the Holy Spirit sitting in His presence and didn't want to leave?

week 3 | Creator of our Passions

All of our passions are God breathed.

Day 1: God Woven Passion

1. What passions did God put on your heart at a young age? How are you using those today?

2. Read together Proverbs 16:3. Talk about who plants those passions and desires in our heart. Where in your life have you been trying to sit in the driver's seat and move Jesus to the passenger side? Why do you think that is?

3. Talk through the 5 Key ideas to reignite your passions. Which one are you struggling with?

Day 2: His Dreams are Larger

1. Discuss Matthew 3:16-4:11. What happens right after Jesus is baptized? How is that moment significant?

2. After His 40 days and nights of fasting, the enemy meets Jesus in the wilderness and tries to tempt Him. Discuss 3 main points and ask one or all the questions for each main point.

3. Do you need to take some time to re-dedicate your purpose back to God?

Day 3: Leave it all at the Well

1. Discuss John 4:1-26. Where do you find yourself identifying with the woman at the well?

2. What identities is the woman at the well carrying? How often do we avoid places of community when we're hiding shame?

3. There is no hiding from Jesus. Jesus didn't want to take the well away from the women, he wanted to strip from her what the well had become for her.

4. Do you believe Jesus would travel through "Samaria" to get to you?

Day 4: You are Uniquely Gifted

1. Discuss the three points for the day. Which one did you need to be reminded of today?

2. Take turns reading the scriptures on page 114. How do we find encouragement for the plan God has for our life?

3. How is God using you to build others up around you?

4. If you're still waiting for the Lord to open doors for you, how has today encouraged you to keep seeking after Him?

Day 5: Remaining is Essential to the Calling

1. What does the word "abide" mean to you?

2. Read John 15:4, then review the chart on page 122. Which area(s) do you find distract you from walking confidently?

3. How is the Lord convicting you to make changes to how you spend time with Him daily?

week 4 | Uniquely Gifted

Our Heavenly Father has so many wonderful plans for your life. He has given us gifts to be used both in the natural and supernatural to guide us towards being kingdom builders. This week we're looking at how we use those gifts in our home, communities and church. God created us on purpose for a purpose. How do we chase after our calling using the gifts He's given us?

Day 1: Staying Surrendered

1. Read Romans 12:4-8. Discuss: What are some of your strengths? Which of the gifts Paul lists in these scriptures align with the strengths you listed? Which ones do you feel you use daily? Which do you wish you used more?

2. Jesus has never stopped desiring to spend time with you. When was the last time you felt that way about Him?

3. Talk about the Spiritual Gifts Test. What were your top three gifts? Which one surprised you?

Day 2: Where there is a desert, there is a well?

1. Share anything that the Lord has stirred up in you as you think about your gifts?

2. Talk about how God wants our time, talent and treasure. Read through each scripture and answer any/all the coordinating questions. Don't skip over the treasure section. I know many people find it hard to discuss money, but generosity is essential to the kingdom. We need to be talking about why our giving is important.

3. Of the three areas: time, talent and treasure, which one is the most difficult for you to share with others? Why do you think that is?

Day 3: Laying the Foundation Together

1. Read Ezra 3:7-13 together or discuss together what we see happen in the scriptures. Talk about how it brings us back to the invitation we received in week one.

2. How good are you at working side by side with other women who God has given similar callings and gifts?

3. Talk about Romans 12:9-12. This is a pivotal scripture for how we are to live a Christ-centered life. Which part(s) are hard for you to walk out in your life?

4. In what ways is your life an example of kingdom collaboration?

Day 4: You are Lovely

1. Recap today's reading in Esther 1.

2. Talk about Exodus 13:21 and Matthew 2:9 and how God uses Esther similarly.

3. Discuss today's 3 points: Esther is lovely, Humble and Wise. Read the scriptures and answer some/all of the questions.

Day 5: Seventy Times Seven

1. Read 1 Peter 4:10-11 together in the NKJV and Passion Translation. Are you planted in a church? Talk about how you're using your gifts to serve others in your church?

2. If you're not serving, is it because you've experienced being hurt by the church? If so, where has the church left you hurt and unable to serve?

3. Discuss Matthew 18:22 and what forgiveness looks like. How does Jesus call us to forgive and how does seeing how He modeled forgiveness change our perspective?

week 5 | In Every Season

We are all going to walk through many seasons in our life. It's important for us to take a look at how we're chasing after Jesus in each of those seasons. Knowing that the Lord is looking for a willing heart, one that is available for whatever He may call us to. This week we're looking at how we find hope, peace and joy in every season.

Day 1: Breakthrough in Every Season

1. Isaiah 58:11 The Lord prunes off the dead branches and fruit begins to grow. What is the definition of a breakthrough?

2. Talk about Abraham and Lot. When have you gone through a season where it felt like you were honoring those around you as they walked in a well-watered land, yet you felt you were still in the desert?

3. How does the story of Rahab point us to how God can lead us to breakthrough and redeem our lives?

4. What areas of your life have you allowed your season, past or present to name you, define you or keep you from walking in a deeper relationship with Jesus?

Day 2: Patience in Every Season

1. God's timing for every season. Acts 1:1-12. What does Jesus do in the 40 days after He rose from the dead?

2. Read Psalm 27:14. Looking at all the scriptures on what it means to wait on the Lord, what do we receive when we live in a posture of patience in every season?

3. What verse about patience did you choose to write out?

4. Looking back at the scriptures we read today, which one spoke to your heart the most?

Day 3: Hope in Every Season

1. Hope is rooted in the waiting. What is the definition of 'Hope'?

2. When is a time you've had to "bind yourself in hope" to God? How did you experience Him during that time?

3. Discuss Ruth 1:1-22: How do each of these women find hope through their relationship? How does the Lord meet each of them?

4. Which one of the scriptures we read today do you need to lean on for hope in this season?

Day 4: Joy in Every Season

1. We need to free ourselves from the comparison trap. Who are some of the women in your life that you've linked arms with? What are the fruit displayed in their life?

2. Read Philippians 2:2-3. In what areas do you compare yourself to others? Why do you think women find it hard to honor other women around them?

3. Talk about Elizabeth and Mary. Where there would be room for so much envy and comparison, how do these two women model how we should treat each other?

Day Five: A Posture of Willingness

1. What is the definition of 'willing'?
2. With willingness comes obedience. When you hear the word obey, what is your immediate response? Why is that?
3. Look at Micah 7:7. Which 'will' is most difficult for you to walk in?
4. Moses - God doesn't call us into anything He's not willing and able to help us walk in.

week 6 | His Sacred Love for Us

God's love for you has no bounds. There isn't anything He wouldn't do, any distance He wouldn't travel for us to have an encounter with Him. Jesus models what it looks like to be known by His Father, walk without wavering in His purpose, living a life of abundance and generosity, even in His short season of ministry.

Day One: Be About the Father's Business

1. Discuss Luke 2:41-52 — Jesus was all about His Father's business. How do we raise the next generation to build the kingdom?
2. Being about the Father's business and finding our identity in God just as Jesus did. In Jesus's three years of ministry there are 30 documented scriptures that point to Him retreating to pray. What does your prayer life look like?
3. Jesus prays up until His last moments before His death, when was the last time you prayed for someone and they found healing, breakthrough or victory?
4. How do you set aside time in your day to withdraw from the noise of the world and spend time in the Word and pray?

Day Two: Jesus Never Wavers

1. What is your favorite story in the Bible of an interaction Jesus had with someone that left them transformed?
2. Jesus walked in His purpose before and after His resurrection. He walked Confidently, Humbly and Boldly. Discuss all three points and how the women can identify with Jesus with each one.
3. Why are you thankful for your salvation? How do you view the crucifixion? Walk the women through salvation message if they don't know Jesus or you sense that there are women who need to let go of some things they've been holding onto and re-dedicate areas of their lives back to Jesus.

Day Three: Jesus was Uniquely Gifted

1. Jesus knew His gifts - He used them everywhere He went. Look at Galatians 5:22-23, when is a time in Jesus' ministry when you see Him walking in the fruit of the Spirit?
2. Turn to Matthew 14:6-21. Recap story. Talk about Jesus's response - what is the significance of His compassion?

3. Why do you think Matthew points out that everyone ate til they were full and there were still leftovers?

4. How do you need to change the posture in which you approach using your gift to serve others?

Day Four: In Every Season There is Hope

1. When was a season of your life where you knew the Lord was calling you into something new, but you didn't know when you were going to walk in your calling?

2. Look at John 2:1-11. Recap the story of Jesus turning water into wine. Discuss what we learn from Jesus about leaning into the presence of the Holy Spirit in every season.

    a. If someone were to ask you if you're ready to share the gospel of Jesus, how would you respond?

    b. How are you living a life of full obedience to the Lord?

    c. In what ways are you struggling to believe that God has more for you in this season?

3. Everything should point to the glory of God. How we live and how we serve Jesus in and outside of our homes. What does that look like for you?

There are five days in week six, but I recommend giving day 5 its own time of gathering together. It's a special time of celebration and testimony. Have the women complete up to day four and wait to do day 5 together.

final week | Celebrating His Goodness

Celebrating God's goodness with a time of breaking bread and testimony. Set the table, have the women each bring a dish to the meal and take time to enjoy a meal together Follow it with a time of worship, communion and an opportunity for each woman to share a testimony of what the Holy Spirit has done in her as you journeyed through this Bible study together.

Jesus' love is so sacred and unwavering, it was that same love that carried Him to the cross. Have someone read John 15:13 (Amplified version). Jesus not only had a great love for you but also a strong commitment to you.

Read John 13:1
Prepare to take communion together. Pass outthe bread and grape juice. I used Challah bread, each woman broke off a small piece and dipped it into the grape juice. Take some time to reflect, put on a worship song that will draw the women further into the Holy Spirit's presence.

Read 1 Corinthians 11:23-26

Take communion. Read John 17:20-23 over the women as they take communion.
Have each woman share a short testimony of how the Lord moved in their life over the course of the six week Bible Study. We clapped and celebrated after each one.

Read the Benediction over them.
Pray to close.

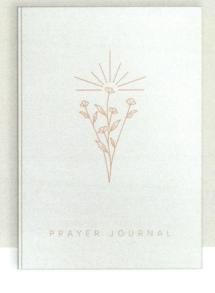

COMING 2023

(Be)Together Small Group Leadership E-Book

Take the hesitation out of hosting a Bible study in your home. God calls us as women to be builders of the kingdom. We do this through opening our homes and leading them through God's Word. If you are new to leading a Bible study, our Leader Guide is the perfect resource to lead you through how to host, how to prepare and talking points for leading women through the (Be) Known Bible Study. In this study you'll find resources, timelines, developing leadership skills, tips for hosting and a step by step weekly guide for the Bible Study.

COMING FALL 2022

(Be)Together Prayer Journal

Prayer leads us to praise! It also leaves a legacy. If you're looking to build a stronger prayer life so you can learn how to hear the voice of God more clearly, we encourage you use this prayer journal as a guide. There's nothing more beautiful that seeing and dating answered prayers you've prayed. Imagine how you will lead the next generation to kingdom impact through the prayers you pray today in your prayer journal. Our prayer journal is the perfect companion to any of our Bible studies.

LEARN MORE ABOUT THESE RESOURCES AT: beknownbiblestudy.com

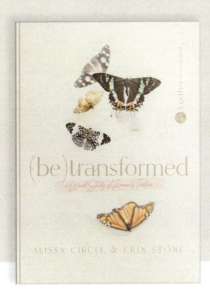

COMING 2023

(Be)Transformed: a 6-week study of Romans 12

Let's be honest: the life we are called to lead isn't always easy. Romans 12 gives us clear instructions for how to operate as a disciple of Jesus — but God's desire isn't for us to complete a to-do list. He desires to transform us through his grace and build us up so that we can build the countercultural Kingdom of heaven with strength, joy, and love. In short, until we get the "who" and the "how" right, "what" we are called to will feel hard.

IN THIS STUDY, WE WILL LOOK AT:

- How we connect with Jesus
- What it means to be transformed
- How to walk in grace and love
- Our unique gifts & role in the Body of Christ
- Jesus as the prototype for loving others

COMING SUMMER 2023

Be Together Cookbook: A Cookbook for Building Community

There's something about gathering around a table with others that brings the joy and delight to creating a dish. I love bringing people together, building relationships and creating connection. The Be Together Cookbook is a cookbook written to help you build community with those around you, centered around great food and conversation. It will take the hesitancy out of hosting.

THE COOKBOOK WILL INCLUDE:

- Tips for hosting a gathering in your home & setting the table
- 100 simple and delcious recipes that will nourish your guests
- Devotionals to share around the table Conversation starters

Be Together Co. is a MOVEMENT of women who want to link arms and build the kingdom of God together. We are focused on Biblical conversation, captivating content, community, cultivating faith, courageous living and changing lives. We want to be women who are known by God and desire to disciple other women into a deeper hunger and passion for relationship with Jesus.

We are a growing community of women from all ages and stages and seasons of life wanting to help each other find and fulfill their God purpose for their life. It consists of Bible studies, Bible study tools, publishing, promoting, producing, programming, coaching, consulting, and a podcast (coming soon!).

Be Together is focused on creating community for new and emerging writers, authors and leaders wanting to expand their impact in the world. Leveraging emerging technology, production, and publishing models. The best ideas are in our community! If that's you and you're looking to partner or build out products and programs to reach women anywhere and everywhere in order to fulfill God's greater purpose in your life, we would love to hear from you and your team!

For a free one-hour session to review your publishing, production, or partnership idea, email us at hello@alissacircle.com with the subject line: "Partner Together"

"Then with a unanimous rush of passion, you will with one voice glorify God, the Father of our Lord Jesus Christ. You will bring God glory when you accept and welcome one another as partners, just as the Anointed One has fully accepted you and received you as his partner."
ROMANS 15:6 TPT

connect with us

- @BETOGETHERCOLLECTIVE | @ALISSAMCIRCLE
- HELLO@ALISSACIRCLE.COM
- #BEKNOWNSTUDY #BETOGETHERCO
- BEKNOWNBIBLESTUDY.COM | BETOGETHER.CO

Alissa Circle
ABOUT THE AUTHOR

God began speaking to Alissa as her children were entering the pre-teen years about the attack on the identity of His people. Starting at a young age, society tries to "help" predetermine how children look at themselves, their beliefs, causing them to question who they are and their place in society. Yet the Word, which holds the only truth, already affirms that each one of us is uniquely created and named by our Creator. We are designed to worship Him, and He calls us by name: beloved, heir, daughter of the king, loved, chosen, victorious, and courageous. We live in the world, but as women of God, not belong to the world. Daughters of the King need to stand firm that we have been set apart to be used for His Kingdom. This book was born out of an obedience to the Lord to point women back to their heavenly father, to not just know, but live into who Jesus says they are (identity). The outpouring of rediscovering our identity in Jesus results in the fullness of walking in His calling on our lives, using the gifts he's given us in the season we're in.

Alissa is the author of the life and style blog, Little Bit City, 'Lil Bit Country, which was founded in 2007, where she discusses balancing family, faith, and everything in between. By 2010, she began partnering with brands to create content on her blog for her audience. Realizing she could be a translator between influencers like herself and brands/marketers, she launched Pollinate Media group in 2012, creating brand ambassador programs for large companies such as, Cost Plus World Market, Land of Nod and other similar brands. Pollinate Media Group became a leader in the influencer marketing space, known for being a top matchmaker between industry leading brands and top digital influencers and publishers. For over 10 years, Alissa has helped hundreds of brands achieve their goals by producing successful social media marketing campaigns with evergreen content still found in top search engines today. She has also coached thousands of women, helping them build their own small business, grow their blogs and expand their social influence.

Alissa is the founder and CEO of Be Together Co., a movement of women focused on Biblical conversation, captivating content, community, cultivating faith, courageous living and changing lives. She is a Bible study teacher, speaker and has written multiple women's small group curriculums for her church. She also has written two five day devotionals on the awe and wonder of God and identity, soon to be available on the YouVersion app. Alissa's greatest passion is seeing women rediscover their identity in Jesus and walk in the fullness of His calling on their lives.